The Scandal of Thought

The Scandal of Thought

Impolitical Commentaries

G.V. Loewen

Strategic Book Publishing and Rights Co.

Strategic Book Publishing & Rights Co., LLC
USA
www.sbpra.net

For information about special discounts for bulk purchases, please contact Strategic Book Publishing and Rights Co. Special Sales, at bookorder@sbpra.net.

ISBN: 978-1-68235-759-0

Contents

G.V. Loewen

Part Two: Some Scandals of Thinking

No pen is capable of representing the graces, the features, and the charms of these eight children superior also to all the tongue is empowered to say, and chosen, as you know, from amongst a very large number.

De Sade (1785)

For perhaps literature and the arts have a permanent function of scandalizing. By readily and insistently representing evil, the artist destroys the conventional and hypocritical image which the righteous are inclined to assume.

Paul Ricoeur (1955)

Preface: The Possibility of a Critical Politics

Any institution that centers itself by reproduction is immediately suspect. Criticism, if directed at the unpolished edges of an organization, edges which either sabotage or yet defeat the institution's ability to reproduce itself, can certainly be found in abundance. But critique, authentic and reflexive, that which calls into question not merely the goals of government or like edifices but indeed their very existence, is something surpassingly rare in our day. Even so, its improbability does not necessitate our own retreat into the impossible. The human imagination is more resilient than any political force. That it is more than impolite to pursue this other course gives a validity to the 'impolitical'; at once uncouth and impolitic as it must be.

In 1933, when Otto Dix painted 'The Seven Deadly Sins', the National Socialists had just come into power. Partly elected, partly manipulating, this regime, forever caught in its idea of the end even in its incipience, raised the standard of internal criticism while at once vanquishing any possible critique, at least within its military reach. The prudent fled or silenced themselves, and it is of note that Dix himself did not add the telltale mustache to the central figure, 'vanity', until after the war had ended. It is a convenience foreshortened to expend the critical breath in one moment; in this we sabotage ourselves rather than any institution. To keep that breathing consistent if not constant is the task of the critical thinker; one must expel much with comparatively little expense, for indeed this is what politics does with its own auto-suggestive rhetoric. Its goal is power, pure and simple, and the means by which to wield that power are to be found in government and associated ministries. Much is said and little done, and the citizen generally knows of this. This is not where the manipulation lies. Rather it can be found in the basic sensibility that politics alone is the space of public thought, that thinking with another initiates a political space. It certainly *can* do so, but when it does, the limits, both upon imagination and the thought that may be germinated within it, are set up quite narrowly, as if we ourselves had been hung up on too solid, unwavering hooks, as marionettes, and thus one step away from becoming true martinets.

In order to free up a different kind of public space, phenomenologically 'opened' but not by the inauthentic desire of our beings to tarry within curiosity alone, one must place oneself at the most acute parallax from the political, and from political thought even as a discourse. The 'guerrilla' tactics of political critique, a mix of the apolitical – as a kind of data stream; who is uninterested in this and therefore who is uninteresting in themselves? – and anti-political – I shall shut myself away from the public at all costs and become the most objective onlooker; the purely private citizen is, however, at best an oxymoron – are well known and inform only the impetus to the commentaries that follow. Far beyond this move, there must be constructed a movement, something that has its own Realpolitik. Yes, it would always be, by necessity, on the move rather than on the make. It would show no loyalty to any regime or any party. It would not be bought or bought out, for it has no price. It *has* no price not because of its dubious value but rather because it is a direct descendent of human thought itself. It is part of the birthright of being human and thus is beyond any price. Politics indeed seeks to place a price upon all that which is counter to itself. The thrust of this volume's efforts is to re-establish a sequence of values within political critique and within what is at first impolitical thought that tends toward the political in its discourse and in its object, in order to aid the self-understanding which says to itself 'I am priceless in all that I do and think.'

The first part of this book contain a series of loosely related commentaries and one scholarly article grouped under the sensibility that any such viable critique that is askew to politics as practiced by almost everyone will be 'unfashionable' in both Nietzsche's and Russell's senses. It is perhaps commonplace to reiterate that the critical social philosopher must choose specific topics against the grain, so much so that the thinker may imagine, and not without reason, that he is the *only* one who has chosen in this way and thence written about that choice and its implications. Politics must maintain its fascist fashionability just as critique must constantly engender an anathema to what is 'agreed upon' or what is said to constitute 'common sense'. In this first part, the reader will find topics that are the 'order' of the day as well as those fashionable in and to their own mind; indeed, these are merely two points on an abbreviated line.

In the second part, the volume provides more in-depth analyses of critical stances adopted over against the perennial rather than simply the fashionable. Thinking is itself revolutionary, and thus like art, it has its own scandal about it, even its own 'evil', and none of this sensibility is docketed or subtracted from the second series of commentaries, whether once again in editorial, essay, interview, address, or article form. It is my hope that the interested reader will take away from these unfashionable yet all the more political reflections a renewed sense of purpose; to value the world as it is in order to change it into being its best proposition – and here, the 'best' is never a terminus but only what is next and what is a must *in* that next – rather than to value either an imaginary world into which many have inserted themselves or a world that is private, in that it consists of only our own personal desires and within which the other is reduced to either an automaton or a tool. If the world holds to itself all human joy and sorrow, happiness and suffering, than its depth is not to be known through *any* discourse that seeks the power to make itself over in its own image, as politics is wont to do. Instead, it is through the reflective hermeneutic that reaches forward into the as-yet unseen and rearward into the experience of the history of consciousness that is a better manner of attaining an authentic politics; one that is not merely representative of a franchise in its fullest regard and need, but also one that disdains power and chooses the truth of the world over its own now dwarfed ambitions.

G.V. Loewen, Canada, 2022

A note on the texts: the two scholarly articles which appear here were originally published in 2013 by peer reviewed journals which over the interim of a decade have gone out of print. Since they are no longer accessible in any form, I have taken the liberty to reproduce them here more or less as they were written.

Part One:
Political Fashion, Unfashionable Critique

Why I am not an Olympian

Canada is objectively one of the best countries in the world. It was a tremendous stroke of good fortune for me to be born here, rather than many elsewheres. But happenstance alone should not engender pride. Canada maintains some good graces in calculated ways, and for this the citizen can be grateful on a daily basis. Mostly civil, somewhat tolerant, with a general sense of fair play and a reasonable boundary of scandal or yet evil, to be Canadian is to be aware of the centeredness of sociality in a manner most other nations either struggle with or have entirely forfeited.

Even so, there remains much to be done. To the ongoing challenge of governing a diverse and geographically vast land wherein increasingly voices are heard across the political spectrum which issue demands that suggest exclusivity and even outright exclusion, one must in addition provide a balance of rights and responsibilities both under the law and within an enlightenment ethics. Our legal system and our ethics are mostly foreign to those who arrive on our shores, and this is to be expected. But that they are sometimes shunned by those who understand Canada as a part of who they *themselves* are is something to be greeted with stringent reproach. There are numerous examples, from the PMO's fast and loose definition of professional ethics, to section 43 violators – almost exclusively parents – to those who at least feign disbelief about the current public health crisis.

Let us not forget those who ape regressive ideologies such as ethnic supremacies, regional nationalisms, sectarian reactionaries and throwbacks, and wealthy elites who imagine neither law nor ethics applies to their sainted natures. Canada has a surfeit of all of these and others alike.

Yet the mere presence of such persons, claiming citizenship but on their own terms, is not enough to pass up clambering onto the epic mountain range upon which the Gods would stand. No, it is that we consistently both deny and obfuscate setting our fellow residents straight on some simple topics regarding both behavior and thinking that forces one to eschew these heady heights. Instead, we tend to distract ourselves by entertainment fictions and spectacles. The most grandiose, and the most dangerous, of these collective distractions is the Olympic Games.

Hitler's film director, Leni Riefenstahl, an artist of the alpine apexes caught up in darkest depths of the valley of fear, nailed the Olympics early on. The 1936 games, from which most of our contemporary hype, such as the torch run, is directly borrowed, was filmed by her and given sub-titles concerning the 'celebration or festival of youth and beauty'. Certainly this is the kernel of the whole affair at the subjective level. Youth is the fetish of all modernity. Beauty is embodied by youth and youth alone. No longer a kind of transcendental conception, taking its place alongside the good and truth, beauty has become an esthetic spectacle, and one that exists solely because of voyeurism and its accompanying ressentiment. There is little doubt that almost all male viewers and about one-fifth of those female witness many Olympian events as a form of soft-core pornography, including rhythmic and artistic gymnastics, swimming and diving, sprinting events, figure skating, etc.. The fact that coaches of these sports versus others are much more likely to engage in criminal behavior should be noted as part of the overall fetish of youth and beauty combined. Not that any of this has an authentic sexuality about it. Rather its sensuality is Orwellian, at once a profanity and a mystery, something all covet and lust after but something about which one must remain silent. It is not the presence of the athlete but the appearance of her body that is paramount. A body put through its paces, a body disciplined, a body beautiful but aloof to intimate entreaty, a body ideological, a body disembodied from both its happenstance truth and its potential for the ethical good.

Sontag's sense of the 'fascist aesthetic', however misplaced when applied to Riefenstahl's visual ethnographies of East Africa, remains absolutely applicable to the Olympic Games. It surrounds us on all sides, as if we were in Minsk in 1941, even as if we were some gentler version of the camps. Yes, *even* that, for shame. Private sector companies flaunt this esthetic with endless posters, banners hanging from the rafters, images on labels, cashiers asking for donations, life-size images of the athletes in question. And who do you imagine invented all of this? The summer games is certainly more imposing than its winter counterpart, but nonetheless, a country like Canada regresses every two years into a kind of 'Fourth Reich' symbolic status. The Reich itself had little to do, at the end of the day, with ethnicity proper and primary. No, it was about creating a new kind of Man, 'men as gods', to borrow from Wells, and this is precisely how the youthful athletes are portrayed; as gods on earth, as *Olympians* after all. A new race requires above all a new esthetic. And this was the simpler aspect of neo-ontological fetish. That it as well would require a new ethics, also superior, conveniently escaped the Nazis' purview.

And it also escapes our own. Why is there poverty in a wealthy country such as ours? Why is there child abuse? Why are there charter schools for the privileged in a nation that prides itself on democracy? Why are Indigenous peoples without potable water etc.? Why do our courageous military professionals risk themselves flying, riding, hiking, diving, on their courage alone? One obverse analogy: The Olympian dives into a safe pool of water with the backing of private and public sector glad-hands. Our submariners dive into the open ocean on a diesel-electric wing and a prayer. Why do many of our fellow citizens desire a *different* kind of Canada? *What*, exactly, are we missing about ourselves that no distraction could ever uncover?

It is the simple experience of inequality; in justice, in gender, in opportunity, in housing, in education, in pedigree, in punditry, in birth, in life and even in death. The fascism of the Olympian esthetic only highlights these inequalities, and for that reason alone *all* athletes should refuse to participate in a festival that fetishizes both their bodies and the State alike. Only when the reality of Canadian life ascends beyond its faux ideals and addresses bodily all of the injustice remaining in this relatively beautiful place should you slip into that red and white leotard and proclaim that your ideal body is genuinely the embodiment of an ideal body-politic. Now *that* would be something in which anyone might take pride.

Replacing the 'Replacement Theory'

Lower birth rates amongst 'Caucasian' populations are due to the gradual development of advanced technical and industrial economic platforms. These require simply less labour power than did previous such structures, the most noticeable shift being between the agrarian mode of production and that 'bourgeois'. It is pure happenstance that the ethnic backgrounds of the population cohorts that first underwent such world-historical transitions were 'white'; a coincidence in the sense that northern climes produced persons with less melatonin as well as an outward looking maritime culture rather than the self-contained massive irrigation civilizations of Asia. Such similar declines in birth rates are presently following along as other nations such as China, the successors to these great cultures, develop in kind. The first significant decrease will be observed in immigrant cohorts cleaving themselves to Western societies and indeed this is happening today, from Latin Americans in the United States to those from the sub-continent in Canada and the UK, to Chinese in Australia and Middle Easterners in Western Europe.

This shift in the character of biopower is sourced in an equally shifting economics, and is thus no conspiracy of 'elites' or anyone else. It is the direct result of an anonymous global process and even if governments seek to control it, mainly through anti-abortion policies on one side, the legalization of homosexuality on the other, they cannot. If the concern is about the loss of

'European Culture', this too is misrepresented. The tens of thousands of young Chinese piano students practice Chopin and Mozart. Is Yo Yo Ma white? Yes, I would far prefer to be listening to Bruckner instead of popular music for ten-year-olds when I shop at Wal-Mart, but I am not willing to murder people to do so. After all, I can always turn Bruckner on when I return home. The hypothetical Fourth Reich, wherein great art leads and politicians only follow this most noble path remains elusive, mainly because art and science, philosophy and literature are by birthright the purview of *every* human being no matter their ethnic background, and cannot be the preserve of some self-interested elite. Defenders of 'whiteness' and 'European culture' today sound like warmed-over and illiterate versions of Nazis and can serve no meritorious purpose in the authentic interest and passion for higher culture of any kind.

As far as the mythical 'Jewish Race' and its cultural interest is concerned, this is an effect of old world property laws that created the focused intensity persons of Jewish descent brought, and still bring, to the arts and culture, as was noted by Marx and Engels in their response to the racist 'theories' of their day, specifically those of Gobineau. It is a happy coincidence for the rest of us, because more or less singlehandedly, these noble people have been the most staunch defenders of culture, arts, music and literature and number amongst the most important contributors to it. Such a list of names includes those like Marx, Freud, Mahler, Schoenberg, Husserl, Proust and on and on. When Wagner said to his virtuoso musicians who surrounded him and recognized in his music the future of art rather than the future of politics, 'You are the perfect human beings; all you need to do is lose your Jewishness', they took him to mean that ethnicity as a category of the human condition was in itself a regression, and in this they were correct, no matter what Wagner's own intent may have been. Ethnic identity alone *is* a lower form of life. But that includes all those who strut their 'whiteness' as superior or even relevant. It is important to note that every person who has been a major figure in the history of art or thought has placed their own happenstance ethnic pedigree far in the background to their work, just as their successors, we ourselves, must do with other such variables; gender, age, sexual orientation, and religious belief.

Instead, the universal birthright of human consciousness, reason, language, creative art, and the ability to adapt to radical shifts in the character of world and history, belongs to no ethnicity and caters to no person. It is of the species-essence that each of us defends what belongs to all, and to do so without prejudice based on baseless provincialisms hailing from the prior epochs of illiteracy, ignorance, tribal and ethnic rivalries, and yes, far more threatening today, competing nation states. All of these represent halting way-stations on the road to a superior being, one that is both human and humane, one that does not shrink from its fullest humanity in the face of shadowy fears of being 'replaced', and one which does not itself fear self-sacrifice in the name of a collective ideal that embraces the entire diversity of the great cultures. For the very best of human consciousness *is* present to counter the very worst; art against politics, science against superstition, love against hatred, compassion against desire. This is its pan-historic mission. Let us then join ourselves to its future vision; a world bereft of the fear of difference alone, but also a world in which authentically noble differences, those that open us up to the very cosmos itself and give us the perspective we need to comprehend it, are recognized as the better part of our shared and mortal lot.

Mein Banff: On Environmental Fascism

While we generally shun the conception of a specifically human purity post-Nuremberg, and rightly so, we continue to indulge it many other aspects of contemporary life, from pet-breeders to horse-racers to hygienic and cleaning products to the idea of nature itself. Given that the Third Reich made purity its ideal in all things, it might serve us well to take a brief critical look at how we have duplicated this sensibility. Indeed, it may be too rapid a validation of our present-day ethics to completely absolve ourselves of even the most dangerous application of the concept, that to human beings, given the rise of a great diversity of nationalist and sectarian movements around the globe. Anything 'orthodox', anything 'indigenous', anything gnostic or centered upon a too-specific way of life whether identified with one's ethnic enclave or one's religious faith or yet one's network or neighborhood, is at risk for sliding with rabid ritualism into the slough of 'the pure'.

One may well wonder if the fetishization of nature associated with the environmentalist movement is both a decoy from, and a substitute for, the indictment against the craving of such purities within humanity itself. The arresting of climate change and thus the salvation of nature as we have known it is touted as a sensibility that all sane persons would accept. This alone is suggestive of a kind of fascism; if you do not agree with us, you must be nuts. And nature cannot be left to its own designs given our encroachments, though national park systems are a nice touch, and most people who can afford to actually visit them leave with some sense of awe; nature *is* truly a radically alien thing and it has not only nothing to do with us it also has, yet more astonishingly to our parochial vanities, utterly no human interest. So how is it that we humans have latched onto what is, more objectively speaking, something that gives us life as a species but otherwise contradicts everything about that life's aspirations to become *other* than nature?

Let me put this another way: the mutability of 'human nature', the very existence of history rather than mere instinct, is testament *not* to our connection with cosmic evolution but to the authentic difference that exists *between* what is natural and what is cultural. And we are nothing but the latter through and through; our global conflict of viewpoints and worldviews alike is but evidence for this. For if humanity had *any* nature in it at all, we would be far more likely to agree on fundamental things which we would then take as self-defining. Indeed, we would not be *able* to disagree, for instinct, the driving impetus amongst all 'lower' forms of life, is of a singular and unthinking force. Contrary to this, there is no singular 'human nature'.

The attempt to frame the wider alien nature as if it had some authentic connection with us – we are destroying ourselves when we destroy nature; this is only a partial truth at best given that culture is itself about the construction of a 'second nature' and the prime manner of distinguishing ourselves *from* nature itself – is a misguided and ethically incorrect misunderstanding of both evolution and creation alike. Whether one is a modernist or a traditionalist – and the environmental movement hosts many of both – nature is placed on a pedestal that - if one is a traditionalist, manifests itself as the truer temple of God; or, if one is a modernist, nature is the replacement for that same God

– takes on the air of purity as over against the raging impurities of humanity. Nature as purity is raped, molested, assaulted, conquered, vanquished, and humanity as impurity is the criminal actor in all of these landscapes. Seen in this way, the oddly diverse allies of nature as are found within the environmental movement can reassure themselves about their own very human anxieties. The person who aids nature is righting an historical, even an existential, wrong, while the one who does not is denying their own birthright. This sounds distressingly close to the sensibility which governed discourse about the 'pure race' and its duty to the wider species. The superior race was to be a role model against the miscreants of miscegenation. It held within its crucible the elements of a future humanity, bereft of all impurities as manifest in genetic faults and mental aberrations. In a word, all truly sane persons would aspire to such a future.

If you are someone who either ignores the call to arms regarding climate and biosphere or denies its necessity, by the logic of the environmental movement you are as were the degenerates sabotaging the Reich's attempts to improve the race and alter the history of the world. Your projects are as was degenerate art, '*Entarteite Kunst*', and your criminality is not even fit to run the death camps which themselves were meant to cleanse us of all impurities and imperfections; to promote the true 'nature' of Man. The environmental state seeks to alter our shared humanity in a regressive manner in that it imagines the 'natural man' is one who shares *with* nature its own life instinct. Is it not enough that we have extinguished much of the panoply of nature's power to enhance our own? Do we now, at the bidding of those who claim to *save* nature – surely but another fascist allegory; environmentalism is the belated soteriology of an otherwise atheist humanity – force ourselves to shrug off the very things that make us most human? Reason, language, art, love, none of which nature possesses, in exchange for a contrivance of Gauguin-like 'instinct' and Rousseauistic romance, perhaps spiced up with some Sadean symbolism and Herodian heroics when push comes to shove, as it surely must.

Just as with those who love animals more than their fellow humans, those who love nature are, with great irony, turning their backs upon their own essential humanity, which has nothing at all to do with either purity *or* nature. If you are wondering about the wisdom of promoting the purity of nature Über *Alles*, wonder no longer. It is simply the revenge of a 'Reich', or *state* of mind that desires escape from its own limited imagination and seeks solace from both the history and reality of our shared, but conflicting, *human* condition.

We Latter Day Eugenicists

Surely it has been an open secret that the US supreme court is contriving a means by which to overturn the 1973 abortion ruling known as 'Roe versus Wade'. Perhaps, with a sense of both legacy and posterity, they will attempt to do so on the fiftieth anniversary of the landmark case. The 'leaked' missal that purportedly reveals news to this regard can be taken as both political theater but also as a signal that the court's neo-conservative leaning justices will only wait so long before acting. At once a signal, value-neutral in itself, will become a welcome sign for that sector of American society which desires a 'return' to a kind of real-time Gilead, as well as an unsurprising signpost for the observer who desires to chart the course of culture-driven politics during a period of global reactionary movement.

Yet the conflict concerning the definition of what constitutes a human life is not, at least at first, a political discourse. In my view, such a topic is existential and also perhaps ethical, before it is political, simply because humanity is first a living organism conscious of its own existence. This is the basis upon which any 'political animal' can evolve and to which any logic of subsequent political language can obtain. Even so, the boundary between what is merely organic life and self-conscious human existence is mobile and notoriously difficult to agree upon. In that, biology becomes politics and in rapid fashion. The question that can be asked of this social conversation, a cultural conflict, a political hot-potato is 'what drives the fascination with defining distinctly human life?' and only thence 'what is the motive behind the sense that abortion is itself an interesting issue?'.

Certainly the definition of what is human has altered, often radically, across the epochs. For social contract societies, to be human was to be *this* people, this group, this community, and no other. As the scope and complexity of human social organization accrued to itself a basic scale and social hierarchy, gradations of humanity became commonplace. Some hierarchies were so gray-scaled as to have hundreds of minute distinctions – several from colonial Mesoamerica included over three hundred 'versions' of humanity, ranging from 'pure-indigenous-rural-savage' to 'pure-Madrid-born-aristocrat' – and even in our more enlightened days, we often imagine that due to variance in both behavior and belief, this or that one of us 'descends' or 'ascends' the exiguous ladder of self-creation. We have neither entirely lost the sense that our enemy is less human than we, nor that my neighbor must exhibit the same kind of sensibility as myself in order to remain fully human in my eyes.

So the concern for defining what constitutes a human life is, in part, a concern for self-definition. Who am I, as a human being? What does my humanity mean? Not only to me but to others as well. Knowing that we as individuals are altered by the course of life in that our existence changes our self-definition – ideally, we would become 'more' humane, if not technically 'more human', as we mature – we also must consider the problem of how to adapt to these changing definitions. At length, we must also confront the denial of existence, that which is not life at all, human or otherwise, and we belatedly realize that of whatever human life consists, it cannot surpass its own fragile boundary. The inability of human life to experience and thus come to a patent understanding of its own completion in death, suggests that we are self-conscious of ensuring that the beginning of such a life be well-defined and vouchsafed against a premature lack of definition and thus lack of humanity, simply because we are aware that this same lack will eventually overtake us.

Seen in this way, abortion becomes an active expression of that which cannot be lived. It is the unlived agency of premature burial. It is active because I have chosen to end a potentially human life before it can take on its own ability to self-define that life which is its own without yet being its ownmost, and it is unlived because the object of my action is unable to experience the distinction between life and death, having not been able to undertake its own thrown project. This seems poignant but it also can become maudlin if we dwell overlong on the sentiment that each of us has a 'right' to life. No, life is a privilege that we give to one another, and that on a daily basis. My defensive driving, my disinterest in firearms, my lack of inebriation, my self-care – doing yoga instead of viewing pornography, perhaps – confers the privilege of ongoing life upon both myself and others. Life as a human being is both a task and a gift due to its historical character and the fact that our kind of existence is aware of its equivocal history. Yet neither task nor gift originate in some other existence, let alone essence. Their pressing tandem represents the very character of the human condition and is not the hallmark of divinity within history. Abortion is a deferring of the privilege of one life in order to redefine the privilege of another.

This may at first appear radical. Yet considering that our very social existence, our general quality of life and the way in which we desire to live – consuming at our leisure, feeling that we have a right to bear and raise 'our own' children, allotting vast resources to defending what is 'ours' against all comers and so on – comes to mean that the lesser other is herself aborted. Perhaps this takes place in the womb itself, but more often it is reflected in relative mortality and life expectation tables worldwide. A rising tide is said to float all boats, but the boats themselves have not been equal since the first social hierarchies emerged. We live aboard the super-yachts of the seven seas. And with this contrast comes the rationalization that the lesser other really *is* worth less, that 'my' children come first and others must look after themselves if they can. This contradicts the ethics of all religious world systems since the advent of Buddhism, as well as similar ideas of the Enlightenment. Paul Ricoeur summed it best: 'The love we have for our own children does not exempt us from loving the children of the world'.

So abortion as a premature ending of the privilege of human life must itself be redefined before *any* other discussion regarding its ethics takes place. We must take this moment to examine how the way we define our own humanity places the distant lesser other at some risk, or yet replaces them with impalpable versions of ourselves, to be counted upon to help defend the front lines against those who would make us lesser. This is not a 'war of all against all', but rather a conflict about the question concerning whose life is worth more and whose less. And however many fetuses are 'saved' or no, it is by the post-partum practice of geopolitical abortion that we will be ultimately judged as having attained a better humanity or as remaining the parochial and incompetent, halting humans of our primordial infancy. Indeed, the very concern surrounding the origins of human life in the present may be understood as a misplaced nostalgia for the birth of our species. To make this the center of any definition of human life in the present day is to utterly mistake the character of *how* we live in that selfsame present. To do so by a political calculation is to knowingly commit to a premature grave the vast other who redeems our self-serving humanity with its lifeblood, drained in infancy, aborted in the back-alley of our base consciousness that seeks to recognize and realize only that which is closest, the closed closet of my overly self-conscious will to death.

Abortion and Ressentiment

> The phenomenal peculiarity of the *ressentiment* delusion can be described as follows: the positive values are still felt as such, but they are overcast by the false values and can shine through only dimly. The ressentiment experience is always characterized by this 'transparent' presence of the true and objective values behind the illusory ones – by that obscure awareness one lives in a *sham world* which one is unable to penetrate. (Max Scheler, *Ressentiment*, 1912-13, [2003:36], italics the text's).

In his perceptive introduction to Scheler's classic extrapolatory work on Nietzsche's concept of *ressentiment*, or 'malicious existential envy', Manfred Frings defines it thusly: "Ressentiment is an incurable, persistent feeling of hating and despising which occurs in certain individuals and groups. It takes its roots in equally incurable impotencies or weaknesses that these subjects constantly suffer from. These impotencies generate either individual or collective but always negative attitudes. They can permeate a whole culture, era, and an entire moral system. The feeling of ressentiment leads to false moral judgments made on other people who are devoid of this feeling. Such judgments are not infrequently accompanied by rash, at times fanatical claims of truth generated by the impotency this feeling comes from." (2003:5). Such a description should be eminently recognizable to us today, as it is expressed in numerous contexts, including sectarianism, environmentalism, feminism, socialism, and nationalism. But these abstract manifestations of collective *ressentiment* themselves tend to 'obscure awareness' that we as individual persons often suffer from the delusions and the fanaticisms of deeply cherished existential envies. Such malice as can be found within envy or jealousy is indeed, 'as cruel as the grave', for it permits us to desire not only to replace the other with ourselves but to see that envied other destroyed. We do not merely want to be 'like' them, we want them vanquished from both society and its corresponding history. In a word, *ressentiment* seeks the death of the other via a projection of a self-hatred at one's own personal drawbacks.

Perhaps the most vocal space of the play of *ressentiment* today appears in the conflict surrounding abortion. In the USA, where such numbers have not varied much for about three decades, 41% of men and 35% of women feel abortion should be banned in almost all cases. About 38% of the population overall takes this line. A reasonable model of human belief and behavior must not only take account of the impetus behind such a belief, it must also account for the beliefs of, in this case, the opposing two franchises; that is, the 59% of men who favor legal abortion and the 65% of women who do so, thus making up around 62% of all persons in the USA. The governmental structure of said nation works to protect minority rights and in doing so, historically may have been said to over-represent any such minority on the political stage. The coincidence of this or that regime appointing chief justices also can lend leverage to specific points of view at certain moments in such a nation's history. For the issue of abortion, this is one such moment.

In saying this, we have touched the surface only of the 'how', and not taken the dive necessary to reveal the 'why'. That is, why is abortion itself an issue at *all*, let alone a political one? It is well known in studies of gender development that males and females are socialized radically differently. As an outcome of these differences, men are challenged by autonomy and fail to learn the skills required to 'look after themselves'. This is reflected in their dependency upon women in conjugal relations and in child-raising. It is only very recently that the majority of men have taken up a portion of domestic labor; round numbers here are on the order of about one-third performing about half such labor, another one-third doing some of it but still the minority, and a final one-third doing nothing at all. During previous decades when men accounted for most of the public work force and almost all of the household income, the previous 'balance' appeared to function well enough. We should not put a valuation on such a symbiosis as was idealized in the 'bourgeois' family, since it has been well-documented that such an arrangement came at great cost for both dominant genders. Both Emma Goldman and Engels are to be credited with the most important critiques of this family type and insofar as it still exists, these critiques retain their validity. At the same time, if men's impotency has to do with attaining a sense of independence, this is nonetheless an ideal of most men. For women, socialized to be caregivers and to *give* more generally without demur, the challenge is to simply preserve their *own* selfhood in the face of others demanding that they fulfill absent characteristics of an holistic self.

The stage is thus set for mutual envy. On the one hand, men resent women's self-sufficiency as well as their ability to provide emotional succor to others. They resent the female's sexual energies and capabilities – no male virility can outlast female 'availability', so to speak – and, at least in the past, their general 'beauty' as defined by the esthetics of the day. Even now, for instance, supermodels are almost exclusively female. On the other hand, women resent men's neediness, their immaturity when it comes to working with others, and their objectification of women as idealized sources of both Eros and the means to ward off the thanatic drive so prevalent in men, who have been socialized with correspondingly more violence than have women. The ethnographic work 'Worlds of Pain' wincingly documents this mutual resentment which gradually turns to the more malicious form of envy. For men, feeling 'roped into' marriage seems a cliché, but it is nevertheless a real sensitivity. They claim to be 'trapped' by the woman, whose own needs they struggle to satisfy in the present-day labor market and perhaps also in the boudoir. Yet the woman is equally trapped. Before ever actual children may appear, she is saddled with an 'overgrown child', to quote the many transcribed extracts, whose needs seem to grow in direct proportion to time served. The freedom and informality of a first date does not a marriage make.

Children are mostly a bond upon the woman. They are thus potential leverage for a man to bring the freedom of the woman to ground. Not only is the cycle from conception to birth a dangerous one for women, post-parturition illnesses abound. But it is to the psychological burden of pregnancy that any ethical analysis must point. Children certainly also suffer from this other resentment – it is no fault of theirs that they are born but many parents are possessed of the sense that children somehow 'owe' them; a clear delusion of *ressentiment* which the old also hold against the young in general – but it is more directly women who find themselves entangled within conflicting demands; the proverbial 'second shift', the idea of the 'supermom' and so on. We are not as certain when it comes to defining what it means to be a 'super-dad'. We would argue here that the men who seek to ban abortion do so out of a patent *ressentiment* against women in general. By extension, the women who seek the same harbor that *same* violent envy against *other* women who seem more at liberty than they. This relative social freedom may be sourced in a variety of socialized beliefs and values, but the most salient variable that influences the relative rate of abortion between groups of women is status in the labor market. Professional or full-time long-term career oriented women have fewer children than meager status working women whose life of labor does not return many rewards. All of us live off this form of penitential labor, and it is global.

We are also aware that the actual instances of abortion vary according to socio-economic status. In the USA this is simply due to the fact that the procedure is expensive. Indeed, in nations where medical care is 'free', we do not see the same widespread attention to abortion as a public or political issue. So the motivation for women who desire legal abortion access is that they wish to maintain this public status as well as a certain material level of lifestyle and consumption, and resent both their misgivings about being potentially self-seeking and thus also less of a 'true' woman. For men who favor legal abortion, they too desire a specific quality of life and may also feel that their dependence upon women is not tied to the woman being herself tied to children. Such men have themselves status and wealth enough to simply 'trade out' this or that intimate partner over much of the life course and thus are not bound to a particular marriage mate who is willing to 'put up' with their other male weaknesses, still very much present. True 'no fault' divorce is in reality based upon more or less equal access to resources, whether these are material, psychical, or emotional and ethical. Given the ratio of urban-rural, educated-less educated, and the distribution of wealth and access to cultural institutions and health care, the prevailing numbers associated with views on abortion in the USA reflect closely such numbers associated with the usual suite of 'life-chance' variables.

While at first glance it seems that the levels of *ressentiment* and accompanying delusions – those who favor abortions are 'immoral', even 'evil' rather than in reality simply pragmatic and self-interested - weigh heavily upon those with negative views on abortion, those who favor legal abortion maintain a corresponding set of delusions about their opponents – they are 'misogynists' or 'fascists' rather than in reality being culturally impoverished and marginalized relative to the means of production – and thus also have to reckon with sources of existential envy which may have their expression in the denial of community or of the import of familial ties. In sum, women who disfavor abortion resent the relative liberty of higher status women; men who disfavor abortion resent their dependence upon women in general; women who favor abortion resent men in general – specifically their would-be intrusiveness through the presence of children as a form of male leverage – and men who favor abortion resent any woman who would impinge upon their 'earned' status and idealized 'freedom' but who also must maintain the means to be themselves relatively independent to seek other caregivers. Though it does appear that *ressentiment* itself is carried more upon the side of disfavor in this issue, we should not be overly quick to clear those who favor abortion on this count given the highly polarized political division in the contemporary USA. Both masses no doubt imagine that 'their' country would be better off if *all* those on the 'other' side were dead and gone. This is ultimately the arbiter of the social presence of malicious existential envy.

Raw, Raw, Raw Putin, Lover of the 'Russian Gene'

His motive was impersonal. He had grasped a great ideal, and he
served it with devotion, sacrificing everything to it, and not sparing
himself. The absolute State was the ideal, or rather the idol, for
which he toiled, the State as it had been devised by Machiavelli and
Hobbes. To raise the country by the employment of its own internal
forces was an unpromising and unprofitable enterprise. He, who was
himself a barbarian, could only accomplish his purpose by means of
aid from outside, by the instrumentality of those who had experience
of a more advanced order of things. The borrowed forces could only
be employed by the powers of a despot. (Acton-Dahlberg, 1906:282).

Lord Acton speaks here of Peter the Great. But his characterization
applies equally to all those who succeeded him into our own
day, almost as if there were a 'genetic' inheritance for Russian
leaders, from Catherine, Nicholas and his son, Lenin, Stalin, and
now, Putin himself. These leaders sought a raw absolute power,
not for themselves, for they were only a vessel, a vehicle through
which the completed State would become personalized enough
for its citizenry to obey it. We mistake the autocrat as some
kind of narcissistic nightmare, as is the wont of a contemporary
psychology that must needs see everything as individual. No, the
absolutist politician is no different from the being who founds a
religion; he is possessed of a vision that transcends both what has
been the political and what has been the spiritual alike.

So Peter, so Putin. Yes, the personal element is one that is
given to both projection and hallucination; one must be, after all,

25

a visionary in order to have a vision in the first place. After the revelation, however, it is all about the person transfiguring himself to match its visionary content. No mere human will suffice. The great danger of any visionary is that he truly *believes*, but once again not in himself, as this selfhood is now to be discarded as 'human, all too human'. Once shed of mortal aspirations, those which are attended at every turn by both hope and anxiety and to which the rest of us remaining mortals cling, the visionary enables himself to drive forward through faith alone. He now knows the *truth* of things, and he also knows what *must* be done in order to align the dishonest world with the revealed order.

In every case, there will be sacrifice. The visionary does not take this lightly. He projects his own special martyrdom on an unworthy world. After all, he has annihilated his own personhood, complete with conscience, and in so doing, he knows he has become a role model for we lesser beings; either we follow his lead, whether as martinets or martyrs, or we die a different death in the face of the truth. For death is now both a release from illusion – the disciple – or a penance for continuing to worship that same illusion – the victim. And wherever there are visionaries, victims abound.

So Putin, so Ukraine. Perhaps a millennia old, this conflict has time and again served as the 'aid from outside' that Russian leaders have needed to make their visionary claims material. The 'bread-basket' of Europe is Russia's golden calf, and Putin only the latest in a Mosaic lineage that understands the same truth and needs to express it once again. And if those unbelievers were more 'advanced' in the old order of things, in that new they shall be far surpassed. The first shall be last. That larger conflict, between Russia and the West, is also about competing visions of the world; *we* have victimized Russia, according to the vision, and indeed, *that* part of it has sometimes been historically accurate, Barbarossa included.

Even so, the visionary is deluded only by virtue of his absolute value, and not in assessing his material means. What he has at hand is not about to be wasted in a fight he cannot win. And yet the unbelievers defend! But since the vision itself cannot be wrong, it is merely the mortal means of establishing the new order of truth upon the earth that is wanting. And this is where things become the more dangerous for all. The means *are* there, even if victory is raw, Pyrrhic. And at the same time *this* is also what is saving us; Putin's vision is not otherworldly after all. He seeks to establish the religion of today, the absolute State, and upon *this* world and no other. He is the messiah of modernity, the savior of citizenship, the pariah of perilous power unsullied by mere human feelings of empathy and compassion. For the visionary has himself been taken beyond humanity.

So Putin, so our neighbour. How many of those whom we know share that seeming 'innate' sense, that supposedly intuitive 'gene' that '*something* must be done' lest all is lost? The evangelical, the 'freedom' fighter, the nationalist, the book-banning school board member, the tough 'love' parent, the demagogue, the uniformed officer seeking 'respect', the 'Incel' male desiring a slave; yes, after all Putin *is* a role model, a model for all workaday visionaries. Fascists of all nations unite! You have only your conscience to lose. You have a world to win.

The Ongoing Myth of the State

How do they overcome this alienated character, this irreducible otherness of the State as the substantial presupposition of the subjects' 'activity'-positing? [ ] subjects can recognize the State as their own work... (Zizek 1990:261).

...the event itself is much too great, too distant, too far in the comprehension of the many even for the tidings of it to be thought of as having arrived yet, not to speak of the notion that many people might know what has really happened here, and what must collapse now that this belief has been undermined - all that was built upon it, leaned on it, grew into it; for example, our whole European morality..." (Nietzsche, op. cit. 447).

Hypocrisies of Humanitarianism

The godhead of the State is far from dead. Its 'glad' tidings are still upon us. So much so that through our participation in the society it attempts to create, we give it our voice, whence it proceeds to justify its actions against us by reminding us of everything it accomplishes on our behalf. It is sometimes difficult to tell which is one and which the other. Its welfare is our sociality, and our conformity an insurance policy taken out by the state with our welfare as its munificence. More and more states are moving in this direction; to provide the basic necessities of modern life in return for an obedience that denies the wider existence of a global humanity. To each his or her own, we might retort, for we do not wish to live like the others. This is reasonable until the rather shallow point is reached that it is we, after all, who make the rules for the world to follow, and in so doing, we are recreating both the positive and negative standards, the worldly thresholds of supply and demand, of citizenship and sacrifice, that animate our European consciousness. Though history itself is far from over, one cannot but wonder if the tensions between the anthill humanitarianism of the welfare state and the dog-kennel beg-on-demand humane society of competitive capital are still entirely relevant. The combination of these caricatures in the world as it is does not defy their intensity. Indeed, it makes them all the more alienating. It is just that this alienation is of the subjective kind, the anomic variety that Durkheim so skillfully exposed and rendered. So much so, that to think at all might place oneself outside the ambit of what we take the state to be about, to give one an air of the *Fuhrerprinzip* in that one might well imagine that it is I who must be followed, who must see through this polar night and thus it is also I who *could* lead my people to freedom. But our self-doubt forces a change of course in the sense that if I do desire to lead I must lead myself back through the apparatus of the political entity that appears to be so shaped, to be reconstructed anew by the 'greatness' of silent grace that seems to animate those who serve within it: "Noble-minded consciousness occupies the position of extreme alienation: it posits all its contents in the common Good embodied in the State - noble-minded consciousness serves the State with total and sincere devotion, attested by its acts. It does not speak: its language is limited to 'counsels' concerning the common Good." (Zizek, op. cit. 237-8). We might well feel that this is the epitome of the contemporary political experience: to serve the state, but in the Soviet manner. And thus to voice our concerns rather than to be the one who speaks, as does the chief of the transient village. Here, no mere subsistence broaches its daily concerns. We are to be high-minded in principal if not in agency. We feel a belonging which apes community because we cannot now imagine life without the central and focused authority of the state. Like a paternal elder, it reserves the right to discipline us, but always and only for our own good, which then can be translated into the common good. Without the state, we are ourselves only partial selves. Our entire political essence is bound up in the mechanism of a center which we cannot directly access, but into which we place both our trust and devote our energies. Civil religion is an apt enough term for the rationalization of this kind of anomie, but its religious character is truncated by the sensibility that we actually share our god with everyone else. Nor do we imagine that the state is really the State, after all, for it is not considered to be omniscient in the same way as was a god. In fact, its omnipresence is more a herald of its lack of ability to either fully control situations that countries find themselves in or create for the distraction of their own citizens and perhaps others, and it may also be an ongoing testament to its failure to reconcile the internecine differences that lay out a mottled landscape of would-be communities and interests. Our own sociality, our ability to interact with others of similar socialization, hailing from similar social backgrounds, is likened by us to a complete society only because it is capped off by a distant but yet predominant organization. It is this grouping of groups that allows us to feel the comfort and security of not having to be concerned about our own subjective partiality, about our own gaps. We then are also able to disdain those other cultures around the globe that appear to be struggling towards what we already think we possess: "... those societies are *incomplete*; they are not quite true societies - they are not *civilized* - their existence continues to suffer from a painful experience of a *lack* - the lack of a State - which, try as they may, they will never make up. [ ] the State is the destiny of every society." (Clastres, op. cit. 189, italics the text's). All the more salient is this evolutionary position given that we actually feel an incompleteness that in fact the presence of the State cannot itself 'make up'. This kind of traditional political analysis underscores both a resentment we feel towards those cultures who are without what we have - indeed, it turns to ressentiment when we realize that they have a freedom we do not, and cannot seem to return to even in our historical imaginations - and a fervor that runs onto the stage to fill the void of our own 'lack'. What we have found, what we maintain in the nation-state is the near end of a political evolution whose furthermost point, receding into the mists of mythical temporality, begins with the introduction of perennially specialized religious role players. The State is thus an annually renewed - however many actual years of office does not matter, even dictators are, at length, replaced - organ of god on earth, a vehicle for the divine powers without which humanity could not live. This ongoing faith in central authority, in leadership, "...implies the unhesitating belief, here especially concerning us, that evils of all kinds should be dealt with by the State." (Spencer, op. cit. 34). For evil 'itself' is mediated by the secularism of the modern state. It takes evil into its own hands, as it were, and the committing of crimes such as those of the 1930s and 1940s in Europe can thus never be truly 'evil' in the metaphysical sense of the term, a sense which is now fraught with *disbelief* and hesitancy, the very opposite of our feelings concerning the godhead and ultimate navigation of the state as the State.

Of course the problem of humanity and humaneness is not at all solved by our mere beliefs, for others have also the civility of their secularized religions, in science and technology, for example, which appear to them to be more liberating than mere politics, but more immediately relevant than other forms of statehood and citizenship. We know that it is more governments who continue the 'old game' of not getting along far more than it is people, no matter the cultural distances. Person to person, we mend fences and live and let live, to a far greater extent than states seem to be able to do. What is it that elevates the interests in living on to the larger-than-life frames of making history? What planes are inclined in that upward swing and swale that allow us collectively to proceed to this 'higher' elevation? For "... if inclination opposes inclination then in the end the stronger inclination wins, which means, today, and in the West: the bigger banks, the fatter books, the more determined educators, the bigger guns. Right now, and again in the West, bigness seems to favour a scientifically distorted and belligerent (nuclear weapons!) humanitarianism..." (Feyerabend, op. cit. 309). Insofar as we are expected to adhere to the decision made once we have attained through the state this higher level of collective consciousness, we must take into ourselves as our own decision the outcomes of such actions. The results of visions made real are certainly diverse, from the depths of the Holocaust to the aspirations of a truly universal health care system or a world court. Whatever their actual content, we must make them our own in order to feel that we are still a part of the machinations of government, that we are still 'self-governed' in the sense that central political authorities, if not actually we in the flesh, must still answer to us simply because we are the 'rest' of society, the brimming masses who do not so much fill public positions as seek to remain distant arbiters of those who do. The idea that we belong to the state as part of the essence of being a political animal entails a tacit acceptance that the only way to escape anomie is to become the slave of the self-professed godhead of political authority: "...this doctrine, proper to a state of constant warfare, is a doctrine which socialism unawares reintroduces into a state intended to be purely industrial. [But can we make a distinction here? Only the politics of a people's capital thinks that industry is ultimately peaceful, and indeed, the capitalist does not necessarily want war, as it disrupts both production and trade, let alone curtails consumption to the necessities of subsistence; ironically, Spencer makes his point by making an error, that the socialist 'man' thinks of the political use of industry, yes, but that industry is geared for conflict and that conflict itself can also become a commodity, so that there cannot be a distinction made in this manner, even though it is also true that it is the capitalist who is relatively *apolitical* in this architecture] The services of each will belong to the aggregate of all; and for these services, such returns will be given as the authorities think proper." (Spencer, op. cit. 50). Even so, this newly minted community of forced likenesses and likes - my new neighbor is *like* me, I *like* him as a 'person', and we share and share *alike*, etc. - cannot entirely 'be itself'. One, it has no real selfhood, and is an agglomeration of selves and others who, in their self-interest and their suspicion of otherness to self, do not willingly form a community even in the abstract; and two, it is not as independent as the modern theory of political agency seems to suggest: "The desired end is attained; the state has won its full autonomy. Yet this result has had to be bought dearly. The state is entirely independent; but at the same time it is completely isolated. [ ] The political world has lost its connection not only with religion or metaphysics, but also with all the other forms of man's ethical and cultural life. It stands alone - in an empty space." (Cassirer, op. cit. 140). Perhaps a less stark description would have to include the ability of the state, no doubt not something sudden but rather acquired, to have filled in the rapidly emptying spaces of religion and other social institutions such as the family. Kindred to modern science or economics, modern politics territorializes in an imperial manner, conquering as well as inheriting landscapes and hinterlands from formerly predominant institutions. If science does this to the older metaphysical chain of command regarding cosmic explanations, and economics with regard to contractual relations and subsistence, then surely politics takes over the roles of authority and legality, as well as the more symbolic suasion of order and paternalism. The church and the family are the largest losers on all fronts here. Even so, both of these forms have managed to maintain a living, so to speak, in the privacy and the margins of the social tapestry where modern structures have not yet extended their reach, partly through lack of experience but mainly because these modern forms bank on the bottom line of interest, profit and amoral power. The highest regard we can have for the denizens of rational-legal authority is that they pronounce a new evaluation and analysis of justice that is unencumbered by the misogynist and network traditions of older institutions based on kin affiliations. This could well be seen as a maturation while still "...asserting that the radical distinction between family-ethics and State-ethics must be maintained; and that while generosity must be the essential principle of the one, justice must be the essential principle of the other...". (Spencer, op. cit. 107). At the same time, nineteenth century correspondents noted with chagrin the same kinds of things we rail against today regarding the problematic enforcement of the legal code and the differential standards or justice within the state. It is a truism to say that some people are ever more guilty than others in the eyes of justice, and that her blindness has more to do with this fact than any kind of actual equality before the law and equity therein. Spencer continues: "...did we find no terrible incongruity as the imprisonment of a hungry vagrant for stealing a turnip, while for the gigantic embezzlement of a railway director it inflicts no punishment; had we, in short, proved its efficiency as judge and defender, instead of having found it treacherous, cruel, and anxiously to be shunned, there would be some encouragement to hope other benefits at its hands." (ibid:124). There has been a slight improvement in the administration of justice, in its aspiration to become identical with the law, given the outcomes of the Nuremberg trials and others more recent effected at The Hague. Yet we are painfully aware of its lingering inability to judge according to the object of the crime itself and not regarding the subject of the criminal. At the same time, we also require that it minister jurisprudence concerning the subject, those 'mitigating factors' which are sometimes called to account for acts trivial or heinous alike. In so doing, we have, rather unconsciously, extended the sphere of publicity well into the very intimacies of our biographies. One of the punishments of a legal system that in fact 'says nothing of punishment', to remind us of Durkheim's famously Aristotelian distinction between systems of retribution and those of redistribution, is surely the airing out in full public view of all of the minutiae of the perpetrator's and often equally the victim's lives. The need for this is as self-evident as the necessity for eschewing such a process, and thus part of the judicial conflict that occurs within the legal system has no direct bearing on the case at hand. Ironically, or even hypocritically given media and prurient interests, inserting the private sphere radically into that public only diminishes the former even while such a process claims to be humanizing the events, to be making a rational process a more humanitarian one.

All of this pushes us further down the path where the state can assert itself as the State, a very much now overfull space where the idea of the private has receded from view: "In the totalitarian state, there is no private sphere, independent of political life, the whole life of man is suddenly inundated by a high tide of new rituals. They are as regular, as rigorous and inexorable as those rituals we find in primitive societies." (Cassirer, op. cit. 284). It is highly ironic that the humanity of being able to share a collective memory of the history of oneself as part of a people should also be hijacked in this manner. What must be recalled, it seems, needs be administered by a superior agency, not unlike the ledgers we used to imagine being kept by God, or as children we thought by Santa Claus or the like. This credit and debit accounting of selfhood and its agency is now the province of banks and governments, tax collectors and lending bureaus, so that its import is purely nominal with regard to the moral sphere. But the more important implication of the taking over of human experience by the state is that it recreates the very kinds of social structures and dynamics whereby the trauma as constructed in the first place: "The 'Holocaust' after all has a pseudo-religious aura within contemporary Israel. It is a central plank in what Liebman and Don-Yehiya have termed Israeli 'civil religion', and thus a vital element of 'the ceremonials, myths, and creeds which legitimate the social order, unite the population and mobilise the society's members in pursuit of its dominant political goals.'" (Cole, op. cit. 142).

Such an order that is legitimated is one that *can* be perilously close to the that of the perpetrators, and Israel is far from the only nation-state that tests these murky waters. Every modern political organization attempts to reify actual historical events and bend them in its favor. The Nazis were exceptional to the degree that they included non-historical or even anti-historical events in their rewritten mythologies. It is at least one step beyond the recasting of history as mythology to simply make it all up, which the Israelis have not done. Given the lies from 'teachers and historical monuments alike' in many countries, the civil religion that recalls trauma to mind hesitates at the threshold of dishonesty and ultimate manipulation. Even so, it verges on both of these things, and as such it replaces human experience with the politics of power.

Ironies of Iconography

This movement leads directly to the problem of the adoration of the state. The nation too has its graven imagery, its official gravesites where the greatest of citizens are buried - Westminster Abbey in Britain is the classic example of this, or Arlington in the United States of America - and like the hypostasized history these sites proclaim, the excesses of all the ministrations or the self-representations of the state provide us only with the means to avoid the direct application of its apparatus, since the state generally advertises itself in such an unashamed and transparent fashion. It is, after all, the only game in town when it comes to relevant public life. Everything that 'the State' takes into its self-consciousness, however unreflective this may be, becomes larger than ordinary life. It is as if the state now possesses the extramundane qualities that the church gave to itself. So much so that like the churches before it, those who are identified with such an institution also not only become larger than life - even if by far the majority of them fly under the public and media radar as unelected officials and bureaucrats - they also magnify, for good or evil, the wider but more diffuse power relations and purposes of the larger community: "It is true that trade has its dishonesties, speculation its follies. These are evils inevitably entailed by the existing imperfections of humanity. It is equally true, however, that these imperfections of humanity are shared by State-functionaries; and that being unchecked in them by the same stern discipline, they grow to far worse results." (Spencer, op. cit. 144). Part of the ongoingness of contemporary state myths is that each incarnation of government authority is an improvement upon those that appeared previously. Here, the messianic impulse of focused power is once again in evidence. This idea that one is always 'new and improved' allows the next regime to plan and carry out its overhaul of various others of its system, justice and correction, social welfare, health and education, to name a few, with an impunity born of the arrogance of auto-iconography. We put ourselves on a pedestal before having taken any heroic action, but we now know such actions will come from us and to us simply by gazing out from our newly superior vantage point. This process of *a priori* aggrandizement is not entirely without precedent. It is commonplace in the sphere of memorialization and subjectivity in its projection of the self into contexts which are actually new but within which we refuse to enter into the authenticity of the new experience. Serial relationships often have this timbre, as we imagine that we can improve our behavior for the next partner because he or she is simply the same person that we already had a trial run at in the past. What we do in our imaginations we also do in life, to paraphrase Nietzsche, and thus we may well find ourselves repeating not merely mistakes of the past - something that we are only less liable to do if we recall our own histories as lived, and not something that will necessarily be avoided in this regard - but categorizing persons as large and amorphous structural variables; the idea that 'women are Woman', or 'men are Man', the 'Mars and Venus' anti-history and anti-culture, for instance. The source of such mystifications lies in there not being an historical source: "In all mythical cosmogonies the origin means a primeval state that belongs to the remote immemorial mythical past. It has faded away and vanished; it has been superceded and replaced by other things." (Cassirer, op. cit. 54). Even if the origin of the world or of humanity retains its sacred aura precisely through its mystery - Noah's Ark as the tropaic space of Ararat and vice-versa, or the sacred images of Fujiyama or Kilimanjaro - there is a double convenience in having it so recessive and reclusive as to be unapproachable. Perhaps this is indeed why giant mountains, especially volcanoes, which arise seemingly out of nowhere and sometimes spew the very dust from which they appear to have been created, are so often seen as cosmogonical sites. Our ancestors were more than content to give over the powers of divinity to these spaces, for after all this is where God or the gods once made their formal covenant with humanity, warranting us to not only live as commanded, but to assume that if we did so all would fall in front of our desires: "But for the modern belief such a warrant does not exist. Making no pretention to divine descent or divine appointment, a legislative body can show no supernatural justification for is claim to unlimited authority; and no natural justification has ever been attempted." (Spencer, op. cit. 174). The uncanny and disturbing prescience of such commentaries must now be read in the light that just such a natural legitimation has indeed been attempted, the eugenics based race theories of the Third Reich and further, many other countries during the same period. Only through Nuremberg did we get a sense that we were headed down a disastrous path, and it took several decades after that to outlaw certain aspects of this experiment, such as the mandatory and legal sterilization of those with disabilities. The self-appointed character of all divine assignation is of course no hindrance to the ever- expanding ministrations of the state. The idea that the world is here for our benefit is at best, only barely hinted at in pre-agrarian lifeways. Our more distant ancestors wrested their survival on a day to day basis from the environment around them, and had no ability to transform it in any long-term fashion, or with any deleterious implications. But it requires more than a Malthusian understanding to apprehend the processes involved in such a change of consciousness even if mythology is seen as a rationalization for the more recent exploitation of the earth; its own version of fascism, in fact, as we work without the consent of the environment and the creatures who live around us, and grant them 'rights' and territories as it suits us. The animals too are 'life unworthy of life' in this sense. If we are well beyond the idea that governments descend from godhead, which surely presents an improvement in our potential ability to critically reflect on their character and agency, then we are still mired in the idea that central authority possesses, notwithstanding, the blank check of power, the unchecked edge that slices through any knot presented to it, while at the same time tying still others that no other body can decipher: "...State-authority as thus derived, is a means to an end, and has no validity save as subserving that end: if the end is not subserved, the authority, by the hypothesis, does not exist. The other is that end for which the authority exists, as thus specified, is the enforcement of justice - the maintenance of equitable relations." (ibid:177). This new order of things sets a dangerous precedent. If power is to be used as a means to attain this or that outcome, where is the body that sets the course, defines the end to be attained, and directs the power? All of these functions and deliberations take place in the same political space, thereby not only marginalizing all other interests that may well be involved - and in our current global setting, all of us our involved in one way or another, and none of us 'innocent' to the effects of our actions and inactions - but it gives those inside of such a space the sense that they are the inheritors of divine assignation, simply because it appears that they can accomplish anything they desire.

So while we no longer associate politics with the sacred *per se*, we do give unto it the same tasks that religion used to fulfill; the structuring of community, the definition of obedience, the identity of membership, and so on. In doing so, we aid and abet the blank check mentality. If government needs do all these things and more, we might imagine that it should have not only the power to accomplish such ends, to 'subserve' them, in Spencer's language, but also the right to do so unchecked. Furthermore, we might also imagine that any institution that can accomplish even some of the broad suite of finite ends and perhaps even a few of our absolute values which we are taught to share mostly through the formal education systems run by the state, that such an organization has a moral and an aesthetic quality that can be admired for its own sake. This unfortunate conceptualization also goes back to the Greek thinkers, who aggrandized their own marginalized egos by identifying their theoretical work with what they claimed were the best forms of social organization, though of course these, characteristically and inevitably, did not exist in the sorry world in which their ideas were not taken seriously enough: "...the state was not only one beautiful thing among others; it was, in a sense, beauty itself. What the multitude knows of beauty is only a deception. Even the artists and poets have only a faint image of it. It is for the philosophes to discover the real archetype, that paragon of beauty represented by the ideal state." (Cassirer, op. cit. 108). At the same time, and paving the way for the new revealed religions in the West, this world was a necessary harbinger of the other world to come. Though it was in a fallen state - and this sensibility may also be seen as coming from the Greek view of the downward slope of history from the golden age to their own - its presence as the landscape of living on in the present was nothing if not proof that the masses could not be trusted to manage their own affairs. The 'affairs of men' then could only be mediated by a greater force whose kinship was with the ideals, and not the realities. Forms of truth, beauty and the good in itself were to be aspired to, but there had to be a role model who was somehow closer to these forms than the common person, who knew little or nothing of them. Plato's 'philosopher-king', who bears an eerie resemblance to Wagner's 'artist-prince', was just this sort of figure, but after the revolutionary revelations of the new religions, such a figure had to receive his appointment from God. This act, the representation of which was a testimony to the leader's relative intimacy with the ideal forms, now manifest and 'embodied' by God's rule on earth, created an odd melange of political orbits, bearing in its decentered ellipse both the Egyptian sense of real gods on earth and the Greek sense of a ruler who had the vision of the forms. Either way, or in this new hybridized combination, the full force of the state lay beneath the ruler's feet, for he could not rule with the aura of godhead if there were not some wholesale attachment of the population to the ideals he represented or embodied: "Ordinarily, the royal splendor does not radiate in solitude. The multitude's *recognition*, without which the king is nothing, implies a *recognition* of the greatest men, of those who might aspire on their own account to the recognition of others. But the king, who would not have absolute magnificence if he was not *recognized* by the greatest men, must [also] *recognize* them as such." (Bataille, 1991:248 [1976], italics the text's). Given that any ruler of an organic social organization is in the end a metaphor for the ruling ideas, the mouthpiece of the forms, and the voice of normative behavior - even though he or she behaves as a mobile *object* in the scenery, the tableaux of hypostasized norms - one simply uses the leader, or the god, for that matter, as a mirror for one's own social presence and movement. It is the personalization of such an object that provides one half of the social bond, while the other half is provided by each of us participating in the mimicry of loyal *subjects* in all senses of the word.

Now if we remove the divinity of the ruler and the personality of ourselves we have the solution to the question of the apparent diffuseness of power in contemporary society. The focus of power percolates through the state apparatus, and the subjectivity of persons does the same through the concept of citizenship. This pronounced a novel architecture upon social relations, as the ideas were brought down to earth and the ideal was that such forms could be made real, and were no longer only attainable in some metaphysical manner, through vision or afterlife or by exiting the cave of shadows. It was the founder of the analysis which understood the implications of this kind of institution who exposed what had really been going on within the spaces of power for some millennia, but disguised by both sincere and insincere reverence for the vertical connection with the other world: "Machiavelli was the first thinker who completely realized what this new political structure really meant. He had seen its origin and he foresaw its effects. He anticipated in his thought the whole course of the future political life of Europe." (Cassirer, op. cit. 134). The actuality of power relations in the modern state allows us to gaze at the old royalty with affection rather than fear. The remaining royal families of Europe and elsewhere are the still living fetishes of nostalgia. They represent what is no longer to be awed and hence can be truly loved. No doubt those who wield real power have become the objects of revulsion, and it would be a pretty thought if we could imagine that this was a lingering and obscure resonance of the period when all human beings lived in egalitarian relations and within a collective conscience. However unlikely this may be, in certain countries today there is an important cleavage between the splendor of powers past and the almost eldritch sense that a political history lives on in spite of it being put to death centuries ago, and the hard edge of rationalized powers that live in the present and commit others of us to a premature death. Between splendor and utility it is the mere flirtation of coy powers that be that give us the utterly misguided sense that there remains a relationship between them. They are alike to casual lovers who dwell in a joking relationship, but here the joke is on us, as we believe there to at least have been something to it, 'all those years ago', and that adds to our nostalgic adoration for the time of imagined trysts, not unlike what we may do in our own personal lives with the old flames of loves gone by, or just as likely, the fantasies of those would-be loves that never quite occurred.

It would be treason to such a romance to attempt to deny that love was never on either participant's mind. But the penalty for such treason is merely the sense amongst one's fellows that one is not playing the game correctly, or that one has taken Machiavelli, or Hitler for that matter, to heart. It is a different thing to cause umbrage to the state 'itself', however, especially if one's revolutionary talk becomes action. Even so, in general there is also no great penalty for disdaining central authority in lands where there are relative 'free speech' clauses in constitutions; which is, ironically, very much unlike the ideas manifest in certain mechanical societies: "In days when Governmental authority was enforced by strong measures, there was a kindred danger in saying anything disrespectful of the political fetish. Nowadays, however, the worst punishment to be looked for by one who questions its omnipotence, is that he will be reviled as a reactionary..." (Spencer, op. cit. 93).[i] This kind of critique which, under the guise of theory, masks an old style politics of both criticism and conservatism, also plays its part in the relativizing of events that are experienced as wholly extramundane. Of course, such questioning whether authentic or no, occurred so rarely, if at all, within small scale pre-agrarian societies, and occurred almost solely through the voice of religious revelation in agrarian ones, that such politics hardly played a role until the modern period in terms of its revolutionary character. Indeed, the structural shifts of immense evolutionary import that occurred in the distant past were accompanied by changes in the ideal realm *after* the fact of the changes in subsistence, technology, and material living arrangements. This is not necessarily the case as we move closer to our own time, where all of the relevant variables were taking shape and playing off and with one another simultaneously. To whitewash the extremities of either structural change or shifts primarily in the realm of ideas such as aesthetics, biology and history, is to willingly participate in not only the adumbration of such shifts, but, if they are judged to be evil, to abet the resistance that these evils have against their own empirical histories.[ii]

The most sure way to avoid these pitfalls is to allay the setting up of any genealogy of iconography in the first place. The use of power must be solely administered as tool against itself. Rather than the revivification rituals of certain kinds of historians, or the subjective anxieties of those who may become victims, just as they watch their peers already succumbing to the authority of the new evil, those who are chosen to lead both society at large and social organizations on a smaller scale must exhibit the fragility of the social ideals of a reciprocity that always over-reaches itself: "... the advent of power, such as it is, presents itself to these societies as the very means for nullifying that power. The same operation that institutes the political sphere forbids it the exercise of its jurisdiction: it is in this manner that culture uses against power the very ruse of nature." (Clastres, op. cit.45). This 'ruse' is hardly a natural one in the hands of humankind, but the metaphor is clear: the symbiosis to be observed in the powers of nature, not always red in tooth and claw but also not always as convivial as a live-action Jungle Book, disallows any species a monopoly of force or too high a density of itself anywhere in the world. The politics of focused power in societies that have broken free from reciprocity manifest their divisions in the new reality of the role of the leader. That is, for the first time, the leader can lead, the ruler can rule. This is the ruse of culture, as it were, over against the once nature of impossible long term or general superiority: "The chief crazy enough to dream not so much of the abuse of power he does not possess, as of the use of power, *the chief who tries to act like a chief,* is abandoned. Primitive society is the place where separate power is refused, because the society itself, and not the chief, is the real source of power." (ibid:154). Insofar as we have lost or forgotten this fact - Marx and Engels attempted to relocate and resuscitate it, Durkheim to restore it through a kind of sociological séance - we are relegated to the adoration of the political magi. Insofar as we have constructed this fate for ourselves - and it has in no way been imposed on us by some external force magical, metaphysical, or even scientific or cosmic - brings us to the shame of having to admit that we have all committed crimes against our common humanity; we are none of us innocent in the face of Nuremberg and The Hague: "This worship of the legislature is, in one respect, indeed less excusable than the fetish-worship to which I have already compared it. The savage has the defence that his fetish is silent - does not confess its inability. Yet the civilized man persists in ascribing to this idol made with his own hands, powers which in one way or other it confesses it has not got." (Spencer, op. cit. 97).[iii] The most common manner in which such an *eclaircissement* is broached and yet even so remains mostly unacknowledged, is through the 'transference' of such absent powers to a realm that mimics the old realm of the other world, of the ideas and forms, or of the divine. The applied sciences of all stripes as well as those ideologues who mask their teachings under the guise of fashionable discourses may be the most obvious agents in this new dynamic which is not so new: "Like their predecessors, the colonial officials, they have no compunction about letting power enforce their ideas. But unlike colonial officials they do not apply the power themselves; on the contrary, they emphasize rationality, objectivity and tolerance, which means that they are not only disrespectful, ignorant, and superficial but also quite dishonest." (Feyerabend, op. cit.27). Through this, no doubt new truths are created, but the intent and the outcome of such 'truth' renders its humanity hollow. One may also question relevance along the lines of ethics, and not merely application. One may question the conscience of any politics that has only its self-interested vision of the world in mind, and theoretical literature from functionalism to feminism can be held under the same reflective lens to this regard.

The power of the new truths not only has an Orwellian timbre, but in their application, whether through the honest but brutal colonialist version, or the dishonestly indirect but just as cruel neo-colonialism within which we are now ensconced, we are able to observe there a full-blooded fascism of intent. For these kinds of truth operate with the view of making the world true by their own means and to their own desires. The world as it is follows along, as it were, behind the truths of ideology and the pretense of an instrumental rationality. The 'truth which lies in power', as Hegel notoriously put it, is a cynical one: "These words, written in 1801, about [220] years ago, contain the clearest and most ruthless program of fascism that has ever been propounded by any political or philosophical writer." (Cassirer, op. cit. 267). They not only have a Maoist tinge, their gun-barrel retains the authority of a superior manufacturer, and no mere political demi-urge. In this lies their real danger.

Unsteady States

Even the most authoritarian regime, with a strong populist following, rallies of hundreds of thousands, and those out of the picture very much marginalized, cannot afford to rest as if it were only an object. Though it cannot object to itself on philosophical grounds or by an hermeneutics, it must remain unsatisfied. No stretch of its limits is ultimately enough, no 'horizon' the thin thread of human finitude written in the crimson blood of a setting sun. Hitler's State soon burnt itself out by reaching for the sun far too soon after its incarnation. Its eagle flew on Icarus-wings of enormous proportions, but their wax had not hardened into the warrior's bronze, or, if it had, other states in the end exhibited an at first hidden iron will of resistance, and defeated the technologically superior, but numerically inferior, German forces. Therefore fascisms of all kinds must attain some form of alliance or network if they are going to survive over the longer term. This occurs both at the most politically general level, such as global geo-politics, as well as between individual persons, especially in workplaces and perhaps even in households of more than a few members: "The widening of the political horizon to include more than a single community does not depend solely on the contingent existence of friendly groups living nearby: it refers to each group's pressing need to provide for its security by forming alliances." (Clastres, op. cit. 64). Originally, we imagine, such small scale groups of like social formations were not truly at each others' mercies, for no such organization could ever gain an ultimate upper hand on the other. It is a different situation, of course, when there are structurally unlike social organizations vying for resources or networks. There, the situations is one of desperation on the part of the smaller and more marginal groups, although elements such as mobility and attendant nomadic skills might turn the tables on a larger population group, such as was the case for millennia in Central Asia. With the pastoral and agrarian shifts in subsistence structure, warfare became just as convenient a means of societal security as did the formation of alliances beyond the level of kin-networked tribes and lineages, as one saw in East Africa for instance. Indeed, alliances for the purposes of making war rather than for intermarriage were in the ascendant: "...that is the perennial improvement in means of violence at the disposal of the mode of security. Improved means of surveillance and control of domestic populations and improved means of warfare have created wider scope for dictatorial regimes and arms races between different states." (Blackburn 1990:100). One of the major instigators for mass warfare was, with agrarian economies, the sudden surplus of males. Their services were not entirely required for the purposes of production, and hardly that for reproduction. They did serve a rather bestial role in the security of the group, not unlike the animals that humans had been observing for millions of years, such as our closest relatives in the larger primates, and other relatively 'social' creatures such as lions. This raw relationship has been muted today through technology and professional militaries, but the hypocrisy of engaging the still surplus men and women of the social margins in either an always potential or sometimes actual defence of a society that has already *rejected* them remains palpable and even shameful: "Practically, while the conflict between societies is actively going on, and fighting is regarded as the only manly occupation, the society is the quiescent army and the army the mobilized society: the part which does not take part in battle, composed of slaves, serfs, women, etc., constituting the commissariat" (Spencer, op. cit. 61). Within the recent metaphysics of godless finitude, rationalizations for this kind of social organization were at first hard to come by. One could no longer claim that it was the other world that engaged and exhorted this one to arms. In the old worlds of gods and gods on earth, no call to patriotism and loyalty, no anxiety regarding the possession of women as one's own unshared sexual object, was relevant, though both might have been given some nascent form in the subjective sphere. The edicts of the gods were to be feared given the worldview which had them lodging and consorting with human beings. Even so, tribal loyalties and extended kin networks doubtless also played a role, as the resonances from the metaphysics yet further receded from our own must have still been at large somewhere in the back's of people's minds. Similarly in our own time, the idea that 'god must be on our side' is still used, though doubted unless or until the crisis reaches a head with most of the population somehow directly effected through loss of life or limb, or indirectly through the knowledge that someone related to oneself is in the midst of the bullets. Generally, however, a new rationalization was necessitated by the loss of the old world in political and economic terms. Religion *sui generis* does not have that kind of sway over any population today, not even those in the would-be theocracies where perhaps it could be argued that the transparency of its use as indeed a political rationalization is all the more self-evident. This crucial new life of the ideal realm's call to arms is systematically outlined in Hegelian thinking, suggests Cassirer: "It was, however, a new event in the history of political thought, an event pregnant with far-reaching and fearful consequences, when a system of *Ethics* and a philosophy of *Right* defended such a ruthless imperialistic nationalism, when Hegel declared the spirits of other nations to be 'absolutely without right' against the nation which, at a given historical moment, is to be regarded as the only 'agent of the world-spirit'." (op. cit. 274, italics the text's). No doubt this imagined world historical destiny animated the Nazis' dreams of world domination. They were not only in the right, but the right was in them.

The icons adored within such a teleological worldview which at once can be harnessed to subjective purposes - the sense that one's fate and the fate of the world are merged is the product of any vision, and the risk is always to those who not only did not share the vision as an experiential event but who cannot comprehend its subsequent interpretations; 'comprehension' of course can be here understood merely as a means to avoid stigmata - are aspects of the self aggrandized beyond rational limits. Yes, one can rationalize the messiah status of an individual human being, but this is generally only a mere convenience, the ethics of which, if they can be called such, are discussed as early as the Mosaic narrative where Moses at first refuses the assignation as leader. Once taking it up however - and Yahweh's wisdom is clear in this regard, because all leaders who *seek* power are not to be trusted with leadership of any kind - he not only proves himself worthy of the call, he disproves his own original understanding that others, including his brother, would have been better for the job. The Mosaic relationship with a taciturn and begrudging group of semi-nomadic herders and gatherers is hardly ideal, but it does set the course, literarily at least, for things to come, For better or worse, "Inevitably the established code of conduct in the dealings of Governments with citizens, must be allied to their code of conduct in their dealings with one another." (Spencer, op. cit. 80). Ironically, the growing power of the new pantheon of once tribal idols written into the more omnipresent language of the State, allows the latter to gain an equally new kind of subtlety regarding its relationship with the citizenry. For to be a citizen is at once to accept the rule of law, and the rule of law is an arm of central authority, empowered to act even to the point of physical violence and perhaps death to enforce its ideals of what can now constitute the 'good society'. Yet "...the strength of the state's new awareness that it could afford to relax its control... [suggests that] Today the state knows that it owes its executive power to religious tolerance and the civil right to freedom." (Gadamer 1998:88 [1983]). Of course the state can also feel free to define and redefine these concepts and their agencies at will, which is certainly always the case with authoritarian regimes. This dynamic, writ small in the households with parents who also desire to exert control over children in a manner code-named 'strictness', is something that calls to mind at home and abroad a sense that diversity in itself cannot be the path to either a true home or a true nation. It might be tolerated and disciplined alike, pending its unsuitability or its triviality, but it can never be rationalized in any ultimate sense: "What we call a nation is never a homogenous whole. It is a product of blood mixture, the most dangerous thing in the world. To speak with awe and reverence of such a hybrid would violate the first principles of a sound theory of human history. Patriotism may be a virtue for democrats or demagogues, but it is no aristocratic virtue..." (Cassirer, op. cit. 239). Here, Cassirer is of course rendering Gobineau's proto-Nazi racialist politics, which, in a clear romantic and oddly anthropological manner, sounds itself as the clearest device for the discipline of an unruly history. Akin to the child whose intents are never transparent and cannot be wholly rational, the diversity and mystery of history also requires the strictest discipline. If history is itself to be a discipline, the analyst must not respond to its recalcitrance with a mere talking cure. There is no time for the 'time-out' in historical time, or in the unkempt biography of unsocialized youth. Yet this reactionary vision of order appears also in many unexpected places. Especially in the effort to cleanse our collective bad conscience of traumatic events like the Second World War and its attendant horrors, the more recent the more suppressed, "...one single, 'truthful' interpretation of the war is proclaimed in academic or political discourse, though another sometimes remains in the hearts of the people. [For instance] As the Kurt

Waldheim affair indicated, neither Austrian historiography nor the Austrian political Establishment are yet willing to admit Austria's special path to 'Auschwitz'." (Bosworth, op. cit. 193). As with high school history textbooks in many key nations: the facts of the cases at hand, but also out of hand in that they are not experientially recalled by the vast majority of any current population, and thus have an ironically free hand to dispense with memory and with history as their editors and educators see fit: "The enthusiasm with which the Nazis were welcomed in March 1938 and the active commitment to Nazism by large sections of both the Austrian ruling elite and the Austrian populace are obscured or ignored." (ibid). This enthusiasm, bordering on a religious fanaticism in both this example and others, represents not so much a liberation of ideas but a desire for order and for a future that can be predicted. Social order is never truly about the present. This is why in part it is always children who suffer the most under the sway of authoritarian regimes either private or public. It is the future we are trying to guarantee by disciplining the present. The *Anschluss* was merely an example of a desired disciplinary routine that could unite peoples in a future-looking history, as well as maintain a useable order emanating from a stormy and half-forgotten past. This desire is partly mythological, and stems from the metaphysics which separated this world and the other world in the light of the latter being ordered, as a cosmos, and the former disordered because both history, being a human contraption, was as finite as was human flesh mortal. The state gradually became defined as the ordering principle which was closest to divine ordination, to the principle of cosmic order. With this, its evils could then be seen as something as mortal and passing as was its own existence. Gadamer himself declares that this is how many managed to muddle through their days under the Third Reich's suasion, by reminding themselves that 'this too shall pass': "The evil of the state, lodged as it is in the original sin of man, is deep and incurable; but it is only a relative evil. When it is compared with the highest, absolute, religious truth the state proves to be at a very low level; but it is still good in comparison to our common human standards which, without the state, would lead us to chaos." (Cassirer, op. cit. 111). This comparison cuts both ways in that one can think of state-sponsored human evil as an encapsulation of what is held within the character of humanity in any case, fallen or no. But as well one can justifiably critique the state against the higher goods of reason and faith which are also given to or evolved within the consciousness of humanity. There is, in other words, not only perspective here but also the implication of a choice that is being made. The usual rationalization of the problem of theodicy involves just this caveat: it is not the failure of the divine that drives mortal being to uncoil upon itself as does the snake. The imperfect world is also a human judgement, after all. What is indeed imperfect about the world as it worlds is humanity itself. Nature and its hosts cannot be judged in this way, for they are not part of the moral sphere. Only we stand within such a divination and we must then explore it with our own peculiar augury, that which combines knowing and believing in the manner that Aquinas and others characterized the latent functions of living within an evolving state architecture, holy or not.

This sensibility comes, as Cassirer relates, from the influx of Greek ideas in the Middle Ages by way of the Islamic traditions, specifically Aristotle. Yet its germination was already available to the scholastics and their followers due to Plato's own inquiry, of which we have had occasion to mention above. That nature was a non-moral sphere was first argued at this point, not only by separating the human sphere from it in a rational manner, but also by denying that culture was in itself irrational, that mind was something that was beholden to a creation that was cut from whole cloth: "This was the last and decisive step necessary leading to the development of Greek thought which had begun with the attempt to conquer nature and continued by asking for rational norms and standards of ethical life. It culminated in a new postulate of a rational theory of the state." (ibid:62). The fragile quality of both the new theory and the actual social organization on the ground needs not be emphasized. Neither would be considered novel today, but we can only witness to the ever-changing and highly charged political landscapes of our own time and know that we have neither a rational state - it is rather, deeply *rationalized* and instrumental and not reflective and reasoned - nor do we possess an entirely reasonable argument for having this sort of political entity and no other. Mostly, as we have seen, it rests on specific cultural and ideological bigotries which we also, unfortunately, inherit from the Greeks and others of the classical period. We may now truly speak of our polis as all-embracing, but not equal in its embrace. The idea that we have the right to speak of this while at the same time deny its reality through our actions in the social world is astonishing to any reason born of theory alone. It may well be due to the disjunction between how power is wielded, the sense of its purpose, and the authority coveted by those who attempt to use it, between our organic solidarities and those mechanical: "If in societies with a State speech is powers' *right*, in societies without a State speech is power's *duty*." (Clastres, op. cit. 153, italics the text's). Having muted the responsible part of the voice of power, we are more willing to engage in the precipitous aspect wherein we feel we possess the power to speak, and thus should be able to do so without cost to ourselves or others. Or, if there is a cost, it is because the character of political power brooks no compassionate influence that tempers its usage. This is likely also why we can now speak of 'abusing' power', whereas in small scale culture any 'use' at all would be considered an abuse. At the same time, mere duty does not impel either compassion or responsibility, because its tendency is, repeated time after time, to become ritualistic. There is, in other words, no real *application* of power to social ills or needs, and thus the idea that power is in fact to be used is entirely alien to such an organization. In a crisis, as we have seen, mechanical societies enjoin their solidarity through the shared system of values imbedded in the collective conscience and embodied in the temporary leader. For ourselves, the regular manufacture of mock crises, some of which grow into real ones, keeps power dancing on toes that care not where they step.

Existentiality of Statehood

Is it entirely a delusion then, that politics in our own time is always two steps away from some form of fascism? Certainly the faith of civil religion is in place, ready to be activated. Certainly the business of political manipulation is learned by rote and by heart by those involved in the secular ministries. Certainly the masses desire to be led by someone they find exciting and even gripping. At the same time, we can take at least one step away from this gathering storm and momentarily question the character of the state's existing at all, given the historical circumstances of its massive failures to provide peace, as well as its smaller successes regarding quality of life issues in the general health and welfare of larger populations. It is not fair to simply state that when government acts, it acts both unreasonably and always plays the role of the meddlesome older sibling: "... the perturbing effects of that 'gross delusion', [ ] 'a belief in the sovereign power of political machinery' [ ] a delusion which is fostered by every new interference." (Spencer, op. cit. 167), is both neither gross, in that it does not effect everyone *en masse* and equally - there are, in most states, conflicting political parties at the highest levels, as well as internal dissidence within the ruling castes and classes - nor is it a complete delusion, because within all of these alternative perspectives, there is a reality to be had. Piecing this reality together may be another matter, in the glare of media, fashion, ideology, and outright manipulation by those involved. Nevertheless, the idea that the State is either a myth or that it manufactures only myths is incorrect: "...we have to make our choice between an ethical and a mythical conception of the state. In the Legal State, the state of justice, there is no room left for the conceptions of mythology..." (Cassirer, op. cit. 72). There is a reality of which the state is not only at its head but is also more or less, and by its own design, both manager and archetype. The dominance of this reality may be challenged by other competing entities, political and economic, such as transnational corporations, non-governmental organizations, and other voluntaristic groups including those quite marginal, such as 'militia' sub-cultures in the United States. Even so, any challenge that is issued in our own times to central authority must be accompanied by a clear alternative to the ruling relations. Mostly, parties internal to the state apparatus may replace each other, sometimes with the consent of the citizenry, and still, often without. The combination of both is also not unheard of, and it was Hitler himself to came to power through just such a shady amalgam of events. The problem of focused power that can be wielded by those who are not directly responsible to the population at large is also not limited to the idea of dictatorial reign. Whatever its from, central authority implies that all else in the realm of politics is but a political hinterland, and this authority can survive even the threat of being understudied by other organizations attempting to gain access to centralized political resources. Authority in reality is obviously quite different from any rationalization of it: "...when it begins to be seen clearly that, in a popularly governed nation, the government is simply a committee of management; it will also be seen that this committee of management has no intrinsic authority..." (Spencer, op. cit. 208-9). We are more or less accepting of the notion that there is nothing that has any inherent authority over us. Norms, laws, morals, folkways and mores are all acknowledged to be social constructions. Certainly the Durkheimian social has great suasion over all its relevant members, but there are many cultures and many ways of being human. Nothing, in other words, is 'sacred' but perhaps the sacred itself, and we remain unsure of what exactly such an idea is composed. Authority in modernity thus has a novel *de facto* character about it. This development aids the also recently understood conceptualization of human freedom or free will in that it liberates human consciousness from the hypostasized bonds of a society 'worshipping itself'. At the same time, however, we have given the State an air of the sacred which people ensconced within its elite hierarchies are often apt to take advantage of. We may no longer worship ourselves, but we are forced to adore the state in many ways, as we have seen. And unlike the great world religions, the art and music of world cultures, and yet also the solidarity of small scale societies marginal to the global development of a common sense of what humanity consists, the State, and especially specific incarnations of it that have deliberately tried to evolve humanity, has in fact not made us more than we were before; it has not made us better human beings. The leaders of any state who claimed visionary goals for 'their people' "....were not equal to the real task of statecraft and political leadership; they missed the mark because they never succeeded in 'making the souls of the citizens better'. Not only individual man but also the state has to choose its demon. [ ] The desire to have 'more and more' is just as disastrous in the life of a state as in individual life." (Cassirer, op. cit. 76). It does appear that in all cases where the leaders of this or that nation have desired to extend the material reach of their powers, they have done so at the expense of the spiritual depth of their charges. Whether through genocide, military actions, enforced poverty, abetting social class systems through the structures of formal education and many more agencies, modern states have utterly shirked their ethical responsibility to the human beings who happen to live within their contrived borders. The demons that have been chosen are negative, sires and scions of a kind of *orexis*, or irrational and unethical desire. If individuals are to be able to choose their own demons within the architecture of modern society, it must mean more than picking one career of wage-slavery instead of another, paying one's taxes and voting, choosing amongst competing brands of commodities, and heeding the laws of the realm. But what exactly does 'choosing one's demon' mean to us today? Can it indeed have any relevant meaning, given the forces just described? Should in fact the state make such decision on our behalf, and if not, what range of demons are left unchosen? "It is one thing to secure to each man the unhindered power to pursue his own good; it is a widely different thing to pursue the good for him. To do the first efficiently, the State has merely to look on while its citizens act; to forbid unfairness; to adjudicate when called on; and to enforce restitution for injuries." (Spencer, op. cit. 127). Surely these sentiments are naive. They assume a citizenry of like-minded fellowship, first of all, where all are willing to play the game and take their chances with the knowledge that some of us nevertheless will cheat. It assumes that those who *do* in turn cheat have the same resources and access to powers, litigious or legislative, monetary or physically violent, as do all others. It assumes that those who have *been* cheated will always recognize who cheated them and how they themselves have been so cheated. It assumes we are all after the same goals. The 'survival of the fittest' is here overdrawn its blank check, it has overbalanced upon itself, and the state apparatus is corroded from within by those who in reality have more of the same thing that most people might well desire.

More importantly, such casual ideas assume that there are no other alternatives in the minds of persons subject to the machinations of state and economy, society and business, and that such people, even if they did exist, would never act on their novel suppositions. No doubt, there are comparatively few of these people, but all governments continue to wager heavily on the inertia of a conformity that they can truly enforce only before the fact, as it were. That is, conformity is always and already a potential mirage, a fragile house of cards where the aces are held up by a supporting cast of lesser ranks. That such an edifice has the appearance of something monolithic is remarkable, but there are generally formulas that exist that can be applied anywhere, on both sides of the issue: "People who conform, who feel generally at one with the given environment and its relations of domination, always adapt themselves much more easily in new countries. Here a nationalist, there a nationalist. Whoever as a matter of principle is never unrefractedly at one with the given conditions, whoever is not predisposed to play along, also remains oppositional in the new country." (Adorno, op. cit. 209). Ironically, but perhaps fittingly, the 'authoritarian version' of the state - and indeed, the sense that there are but guises of authoritarianism rather than guises of states is the more likely understanding of political reality - seeks more than anything else to reduplicate not only itself but the long-lost solidarity of mechanical societies. To be a citizen is to be the same thing in the eyes of the State. And in those eyes, like those of the previous godhead, all are seen as equals. To defy such an edict is to relinquish citizenship, with all its security and sentiment, with all its pretense at solidarity and community, and with all the loyalty due to oneself that an individual can command of his or her country. If the state demands that we 'look not for what our country can do for us', this cynical rhetoric blinds us to the fact that what each country asks us to do for itself means the ultimate sacrifice of one's individual 'demon'. Patriotism, although it is at one level merely loyalty made into the claptrap of nationalist propaganda, is also at another level the key to life within the dominant political landscape of our times. We must adhere to what the State demands, even though there may be some small interstices in its framework where an individual can escape for a time and be by oneself. Even so, an injury, physical or mental, must be treated. An unemployed person must find work, and a child must be educated. If we share, at a great distance, the desire for a solidarity and community that linked our ancient ancestors, we also are fated to share their plaintiff that authentic individuality must at length escape us as well: "In the end, what the songs of the Guayaki Indians bring back to us is that it is impossible to win on all fronts, that one cannot but respect the rules of the game, and that the fascination of non-participation entices one to a great illusion." (Clastres, op. cit. 124).

In spite of this tension, our sociality, our very humanity, commits us to not merely playing the game and thus of course being played by it, but as well understanding it *as* a game created by and for ourselves. It not only represents our humanity, it encapsulates it. It also essentializes it, perhaps in a too reificatory manner, but it nonetheless is more than a symbol for who we consider ourselves to be: "The state originates in the social instinct of man. It is this instinct that first leads to family-life and from there, in a continuous development, to all the other and higher forms of commonwealth. It is, therefore, neither necessary nor possible to connect the origin of the state with any supernatural event." (Cassirer, op. cit. 114). Whether we look to Aquinas or Engels, utterly different in their metaphysics, there is the sense that the frameworks of human community are not based on anything but themselves. Therefore we must take full responsibility for their failures, whether in the home or in the nation, whether as specific face to face relations with other individuals, or on the global scale amongst competing states. What these metaphysics are implying is that there is an ethical onus that we must honor, that we live in the time of humanity and its communities and absences thereof, and that we also live with a conception of time 'itself' that is also a human invention: "They understand the term 'origin' in a logical sense not in a chronological sense. What they are seeking for is not the beginning, but the 'principle' of the state..." (ibid:173). If this principle be unity, be at first the mimicry of the 'One' which dwells in the realm of forms, indeed of the principles 'themselves', then we do have our connection between the solidarities of human chronology. As Clastres suggests, the difference lies in their valuation of this idea of unity. Small scale societies say that it is evil, and larger scale ones good. This makes sense insofar as the larger the scale, the more likely division is to develop. The larger scale cultures need to believe in the goodness of the One because through it they can remain together. Since small scale cultures already are unified in their rejection that there needs to be a representation of the collective conscience in a person or a position, they associate this oneness with a negative force, a force which would impel dissolution of the solidarity they already have *and can maintain* without symbolic reference precisely due to its small scale: "...prophetism is the heroic attempt of a primitive society to put an end to unhappiness by means of a radical refusal of the One, as the universal essence of the State." (Clastres, op. cit. 217). Given that such discomfort must only be sensed - and one wonders in what experience could the members of a mechanical solidarity have sensed it at all; in a word, where does the sense of symbolic oneness come from given their social conditions? - because if it was actually realized it would be too late, the idea that any symbolic representation of unity could thence become more than symbolic, could in fact wield the power of the group by itself and for itself, is highly prescient. We might well imagine that it was through warfare and other conflicts with other groups, and even perhaps the factionalism of certain kin relations within small groups, that gave our apolitical ancestors the clue they needed to avoid following through on these 'opportunities'. The victory over the next village may have given the glimpse of political power, in the concentration of the two into the one. The polygyny of certain family groups may have exhibited a kind of superior oneness to contemporary observers. However this may be, it is startling that the scale of society 'itself' demands that such glimmers of accumulated resources and power be enacted on a wider and more realistic scale, that they no longer remain in the fantasies of those who flirt, but never seriously enter into a courtship, let alone a marriage, with them: "Be it or be it not that Man is shaped in iniquity and conceived in sin, it is unquestionably true that Government is begotten of aggression and by aggression. In small undeveloped societies where for ages complete peace has continued, there exists nothing like what we call Government: no coercive agency, but mere honorary leadership, if any headship at all." (Spencer, op. cit. 79). *The reality of unity in mechanical solidarity can afford to deny any symbolic form thereof. The reality of division in organic solidarity cannot afford to let go any symbolic unity it may construct therein.* This is the kerygmatic quality of the theme we are receiving from an evolutionary or a non-evolutionary analysis alike.[iv] If this be the case, one must either decide to let go of essential individuality as an existential affair of the heart, as it were, as a self-concern which tends towards both vanity and compassion, or to strike out literally on one's own, become the unity oneself and thus also participate fully in both the ultimate vanity - that the single human being is in fact all that is necessary for the essence of oneness to take hold - and concernful being - in that it is due to one's ethics that all are part of oneself and that oneself is part of all others and this thus generates the higher and essential unity.

Either way, one must shed one's actual and symbolic bigotries, and in the end, this is not truly possible, given that the ideas themselves from which unity are derived, the very observations of power at work and at rest, must come from specific cultures and specific histories that we call our own. We do not know any other histories that may have been, the 'universality' of the human condition is but a moot point, though a convenient starting point for both an ethics of humanity but also for yet more bigotry: "We shall go no further than to reject what ethnocentrists take for granted: that the bounds of power are set by coercion, beyond which and short of which no power would exist. In fact, power exists [ ] totally separate from violence and apart from any hierarchy." (Clastres, op. cit. 22). The great myth of power's power, as it were, comes from the bias that empowers us to see it only in the coercive form that is dominant today. Its very dominance may be ascribed to our willingness to let it symbolic dominate us in the manner we have grown accustomed to since birth. Because its reach is as striking as its ability to disregard other symbolic systems which once claimed to have a coerciveness of their own, it appears that it is not merely a question of one system of signs supplanting another, taking from it the power that already was extant rather than transforming the character of power itself. But this is indeed an appearance, and the root condition for its ability to maintain and reproduce itself over the modern period is likely the existence not so much the immediately and irredeemably fascist architecture of the modern nation state as its rational-legal character, its emplacement in a sphere of *amorality*: "...the modern state erodes traditional moral concepts. [ ] The will of the state rewrites moral rules. The Holocaust shows that no moral rule is sacrosanct. Even the most traditional moral canon falls before the presence of unlimited Power." (Glass, op. cit. 130). And it is hardly the weight of tradition alone that adjudicates whether this or that moral system is worthy of our notice, let alone our obedience or adoration. In fact, the powers of other realms which are inherently non-moral have carried moralities along with them as either handy rationalizations - The Nazis invented a new morality for their deeds, just as did the ancient Hebrews for their mythological triumphs; in other words, it is not morality *per se* that guides the world of action as recorded by history - or as the dross of other more structural items that were borrowed or absorbed in the confluences of culture history. Those who run the state apparatus transmit their already moral will into the juggernaut that will vanquish all other morals. It is our contemporary lot to either suffer or gain from the state's ability to 'rewrite moral rules', to image the other in its own image, but in previous ages there were other institutions that did so with equal aplomb. so there is nothing to be gained by pining for traditions which themselves had all of the organic forces focused within them and could act with the same fascist impunity against competing or conflicting moral systems.[v] What we must take away from such a plaintiff is no nostalgia, but a renewed vigilance that it is also our contemporary lot to be, not guardians of morality at all costs, but adjudicators of morality; to be those who also value *revalued* systems of values, and not let the state, or any other single organization of power, do for us this essential task.

Veni, Vidi, Vichy?

From 1940-1944 Vichy was the ignominious puppet government for the Third Reich's occupation of France as a whole. Consisting of collaborators, it toppled during the allied liberation of that part of Europe. In one of its few acts of humanity, it allowed one specific prisoner of war camp to become the only degree granting agency within the universe of camps that erupted across the continent like a radically metastasized cancer. This camp housed many important young intellectuals of the day and well beyond, including Mikel Dufrenne and Paul Ricoeur. The latter's late work concerning the concept of justice and problem of historical forgiveness is no doubt testament to the time he served in such a place.

But after two decades of time served in Afghanistan, what is the character of forgiveness here? No anti-Taliban Afghan would forgive us, for example. We abandoned them to a fate which was not at all preordained, though it will prove fatal to any possible vision which the vast majority of that country's people might have begun to foster. Overnight, their culture regressed approximately 2.6 millennia. In a word, returned to the barbarism and blight of the pre-generalized ethics predating the trinity of newer Agrarian epoch religious world systems, Buddhism, Christianity, and Islam. Yes, the Taliban claim to be Islamic, but this is a veneer, a convenient hat to wear, even a mask of gentility, perhaps. What they are is what all marginalized and neo-colonialized groups are: the mostly rural peasantry of a mode of production long surpassed in both discourse and geo-politics but stubbornly hanging about in the lands thus far forsaken by both capitalism and humanism alike.

For previous to the advent of Buddhism, agrarians lived in caste systems that naturalized the sense in which certain classes of persons were deemed to be at best irredeemable – at least in their present incarnations – and at worst sub-human, even non-human. Hindu-Dravidian, Egyptian-Judaic, and Greco-Roman systems were quite honest about the hierarchy of pedigrees animating human beings. Slavery was a given in the West for example, with no need to justify it until the world of ideas began to slowly alter its course from mythos to logos. Even so, within each of these earlier trinities of Agrarian epoch belief systems the seeds for a common ethics and a universal understanding of one's fellow human as not simply *akin to* oneself, but as another to self, as *kindred with* self, were present. These would include the origins of the scientific worldview in Greece, the sense of moral weight within a life lived in Egypt, the relative equality of intimacy between the dominant sexes in India, the idea of a deity with a human, historical interest in ancient Hebrew thought, and so on. Even if the inertia of traditions dies hard, the very idea that in 2021 one could even think about a state that runs itself through such ancient and surpassed self-understanding is almost beyond the imagination.

And yet it remains as real. Today, women and children are the key chattel of yesteryear's morals, and the reason why the abandonment of Afghanistan is so hard to bear in the West at least is that it exposes part of our own belief system for what it is. For as did Death dwell in Arcadia, the Taliban also dwell among us.

From Texan and Polish anti-abortion laws, to the absence of domestic abuse laws in Russia, to the lack of potable water for many Indigenous Peoples in Canada, to the physical coercion of children in East Asia and the United States and some few parts of Europe alike, not to mention the racial and ethnic inequalities pervading almost all large political regions, it is clear that the more ancient rubrics of what constitutes not only human life, but a moral life, resonate from far beyond their collective historical grave. Anywhere we observe ourselves disdaining the other not for what she is as a person but for what she supposedly represents as a *type*, we are practicing those pre-generalized moralities of the earlier agrarian trinity. The abhorrence of slavery, which is itself a very recent sensibility and one not at all universally shared, should not blind us to our adherence to more informal practices of servitude, from bullying and lying to our children to the idea of private property and everything in between. It is sage to recall that nary a hierarchy is left standing with the newer ethics. Forbearance, the love of one's enemies, the castigation of false prophets and prophecies alike, combined themselves in a trenchant and lasting historical critique of the civilizations that had rested upon the idea that there really were different types of human beings out there, to the point of those on the bottom requiring nothing and being 'life unworthy of life', to borrow a Nazi favorite.

In Afghanistan, young women in particular are so unworthy. But is it all that different for us? The tortured amalgam of our adoration of youth and yet our obsessive controlling of youth speaks to the same morality of ownership that was given its most grandiose forms in the culmination of the first sedentary civilizations. I worship you but you are mine nonetheless. You should be grateful to me for my affections, for an affection is all you are, in the end. An object of desire, a subject of my domain, pretty is as pretty does.

Now the explanation for our abandonment of 'them' comes into focus. This is not a mere convenience of politics, let alone some euphemism for 'tough love' – these countries need to look after their *own* problems, god dammit – nor is it a simple logistical failure in the face of a mere one-hundred thousand mostly pedestrian fighters who have nothing to lose in any case. All of these are symptomatic rather of a loss of determination, which is also the first sign of a yet deeper malaise: we are yet tempted by the *same* morality that has overtaken marginal Afghanis and created through them the Taliban and like forces. It works for us at a personal level – as small as is my life, thank god I'm not someone like *him* – and it works at the cultural level – for instance, youth needs to be sanctioned and molded into passive producers-consumers. In a word, it is *we* who are the primary source of unworthy life in this world, not a bunch of ex-peasant illiterates who have little grasp of the faith they claim membership in. For how can the West provide a role-model to the otherness of the world at large by reproducing social status and wealth hierarchies at pace, continuing to treat its children and youth as only partial humans with correspondingly partial human rights, and vehemently envisioning women as the uninscribed obelisks of phallic desire? (You are any man's prize, you are thus *every* man's prize). Our schools, the fashion system, the family, the sporting life, and even some of our legal codes continue to pay heed to the morality that states with certainty that some people are not worth as much as others, and that some fewer people, perhaps, may even be utterly worthless.

It was clearly not 'worth' *our* while to stick around protecting the youth of Afghanistan, of all places. The boys can become fodder for future conflicts, temporarily served by the girls who are to become enslaved to them in all ways. This more or less *was* the world before Prince Gautama had his revelation, and after over two and half millennia of conflicting values and histories, cultures and persons, we may well ask why we have ourselves become the latest Vichy government, collaborating not quite passively with the slavers, the murderers, the authoritarians, and most disturbingly, the old-world moralists of myth and inhumanity alike.

Will the Real Feminists Please Stand Up!

> The state exacts the utmost degree of obedience and sacrifice from its citizens, but at the same time treats them as children by maintaining an excess of secrecy, and a censorship of news and expressions of opinion that renders the spirits of those thus intellectually suppressed defenceless against every unfavourable turn of events and every sinister rumour. It absolves itself from the guarantees and contracts it had formed with other states, and makes unabashed confession of its rapacity and lust for power, which the private individual is then called upon to sanction in the name of patriotism. (Freud, 1957:293-4 [1915]).

With the news of the imminent return of Afghanistan to the dreaded and derided Taliban, in spite of two decades of war and some 830 *billions* of dollars in funding, equipment and training, of thousands of casualties, of rapine and murder and mayhem that makes the usual business of warfare appear nonchalant, in spite of all of the hand-wringing and head-scratching and the ignoring of history, one receives, along with all of this other disbelief, the truer message of the stakes; that 'this is a war on women and the world is watching it happen'. This is the claim now making its way into media and I think it lies near the essence of the conflict, which is in fact a global one. If one takes such a claim seriously, then can it be but tantamount to a call to arms?

Alexander 'the great' is still considered by many military historians to be the best leader of his kind known to history. Though he carved out a vast empire, introduced the idea of cosmopolitan into the world, exhorted both trade in resources but also in ideas, and saw the city named for him blossom into the most important cultural center of the day, including its famed library, taking his triumphs all the way from Egypt to India, yet he took one look at Afghanistan and said, 'forget it'. This was well over 2300 years ago. Ever since, lesser leaders and lesser generals, though with equally brave soldiers, have attempted to prove their apical ancestor wrong, with dire results. It is difficult to not view the current cataclysm as both a giving up as well as a giving in.

But if this conflict is really about the oppression of women by men, then where is the army of feminists to counter it? And, we might ask more generally, why is there not such a force already in existence? The USA has 'Blackwater', for instance, and Russia has, rather ironically, 'Wagner', and so on. So where is 'Hypatia', as I am going to name it, though it does not yet exist? Where is that just force of women who are willing to actually fight for their global sisters, lay down their lives for them in a fifth wave of feminism that moves from the activist and somewhat *ad hoc* fourth wave to a true mercenary machine? How many liberated women are there, actually, in the world today, who have the prescience, the skills, and the simple guts to take on the likes of the Taliban? There is nothing about modern military equipment that would defeat a healthy woman's physique. This is no problem of logistics, or even 'bias'. Women can fight just as well as men, and by the gods do they have a greater cause.

The idea that, on the one hand, this is a war against women, which it surely at least in part is, and the sense, on the other, that these same women can appeal to nation-states so aptly described by Freud near the start of the First World War, led mostly by men and staffed mostly by men and protected by soldiers who are almost exclusively male, is nothing less than ludicrous. If this *is* truly a woman's fight first and foremost, then Hypatia, an organization which should exist in principle, without respect of country, creed, or credit, must needs destroy the Taliban and all like them, globally and without mercy, to the very last devious, disgusting, desperate but also lost soul of man. For women to be authentically liberated means the closing of cathedrals, the jacking of gestation, the banning of burlesque, the hacking of all hackneyed hooks telling us that women are and thus can be *only* beautiful or nurturing, only either Eve or Mary, the seducer or the redeemer and it is thus men, and only men, who *act* in the world as it is. And what action we may all of us so readily observe.

So if those who claim to be feminists won't say it, it falls to the middle-aged white male European philosopher to do so. That is, the scion of the history of Western consciousness, the very source of all that *is* feminist in this yet medieval world of ours, the space and place of general human freedom, unimaginable in other cultures, and the well-spring of the better future which still believes in not only the individual, but also her utterly human ability to act and work in the world of acts and works which only appears to be masculine and yet which desires, as with all masculinity, to rape itself into a self-loathing from which no one, woman or man, will ever escape.

The Impersonal is not the Apolitical

> One could thus say that history is action in the realm of the imaginary, or even the spectacle that one gives oneself of an action. Conversely, action consults history, which teaches us, says Weber, certainly not what must be willed, but the true meaning of our volitions. (Merleau-Ponty, 1955:11).

Recently the activist slogan 'the personal is the political' has become well known to anyone who has attempted to identify themselves and thus their actions with a cause. This 'volition', this being-for-something, has a number of meanings as well as manifestations. And it is to its own history – the act that has been and not the action which will be – that we must look to find the pedigree of interconnected meanings which have accrued to this or that sensibility regarding our actions in the present. Weber is the first to thoroughly understand this relationship, which originates as an horizon of expectations and associated historical lenses in Vico by 1725. For it is in the distinction between finite goals and absolute values that we discover both action and act in tandem and as mutually imbricated.

Let us first examine our sense of what constitutes 'the personal'. For the Greeks, the purely private person was termed the 'idiot', the one who turns his back upon not only his civic duties but sociality in general. We could, with perhaps a mere footnote, continue such a use of this term today. But other Greek terms are more expansive and collide more forcefully with our modern horizon of meaningful expectation. The person who flouts social custom and morality is the 'moron'. Such a term is in scant use today, at least in polite circles, but its general meaning is well taken. Of course, yet more obscure now is the Greek's term for the one who flouts the fates themselves; he is nothing less than the 'hypermoron'. But we can safely disregard this bold individual given the altered meaning of destiny in modernity. We do, however, still understand those who simply don't seem to 'get it', whether the scene is civility, sociality, citizenship or yet domesticity or the work life, as being not merely abnormative culturally but also somehow beyond the social succor of mutual aid. 'They don't *want* to fit in', is something we hear of such fellowmen, with the heavy ellipsis that we should, in our turn, feel no sympathy for them since, in their 'moronic' action they add to the stress and strain felt by the remainder of us who continue to labor for a sane society and a healthy humanity.

At the same time, we are aware of the tension between the individual and the group, the citizen and the state, the person and the polis. It seems to us a perennial one but in fact it is scarcely three centuries old. The 'sovereign' individual of the Enlightenment remains a Western ideal, even though personal rights are either questioned or yet limited in many places globally. But even in the West, we are shy of declaring the fullest range of human rights to the singular self simply because no society could exist without some certain set of limitations placed upon that same selfhood. These boundaries are under constant scrutiny and have been found to be most mutable, for better or for worse. And since the individual cannot ever be entirely free of obligation to the group, another modern distinction has come to the fore; that between public and private.

It is in Arendt that we find the deepest exposition of the relationships between the public life of a member of the polis and the privacy of that same *person's* alternate domain. Mirroring in a kind of 'material' manner the much more ancient distinction between the life of contemplation and the life of action, the one today understood as personalist and even private – though not in the utter disregard for either the public life or its 'action' – and the other observed in the shared sphere of the 'open space' of the public. It is this further division between how others may or may not interact with the person who has committed her thoughts to the private sphere and equally been committed to her actions in the collective realm that gives us the impression that we have inevitably and necessarily divided *ourselves* into two patently differing parts. Psyche and Anthropos, soul and form, mind and body, person and persona and so on, all cleave to this contemporary sense – and is it not also a sensation? – that I am not one thing entire but rather two relatively discreet entities; my 'truer' self and what I show to the world.

Certainly at this point it can be gainsaid that both such conceptions of the self are 'true' in that they have both validity – a conceptual forcefulness and sensibility that includes both fact and value – and veridicity – that they are convincing enough to generate a portion of our worldview or social reality. When we casually, but regularly, tell someone that 'this is a personal matter', we are speaking over the divide that speaks between these two major aspects of modern selfhood. In due course, much of what may have been occluded comes to wider light, whether in politics or in biography. This tells us that the personal is time sensitive. Something overfull with meaning at one point in our lives may even become devoid of relevant meaning later on. Each of us, having lived long enough, will experience many such transitions, which in turn tell us that the apparently discrete division between private and public, personal and impersonal, is at the least quite mobile and its discretions are liquid. Both of these characteristics impinge on any sense that in principle, 'the personal *is* the political', that is, always is so.

Clearly, in fact, it is not. Indeed, as vouchsafed by the vast majority of social media posts, what people take to be personal and yet are avidly interested in sharing with certain others is hardly political in nature and never will become so. Now one may argue, with Baudrillard for instance, that the oft perverse simulacra constructed by and through digital life is after all representative of a kind of politics, the oddly but fittingly also perverse 'politics of the apolitical', shall we say. This suggestion is not without merit, but it remains a distortion of the widely shared social meaning of that which the polis consists: the collective identity and obligation of a culture as made manifest by the members thereof. Insofar as digital pedantry documenting the innumerable and seemingly interminable quotidia of the daily round is neither collectively identified with – witness the digital cliques often in conflict with one another – nor is anyone obligated to pay any attention thereto, these 'persona of personalism' remain outside meaningful political thought and action alike.

The same cannot be said for the impersonal. Let us now turn to this obverse concept. If the 'personal' cannot be either 'idiocy' or 'publicity', and we have suggested it cannot in principle and by definition as well be the political, the 'impersonal' appears to escape all of these limitations in one stroke. One, the impersonal is manifest not in individuals at all but rather in social institutions, such as the church, the state, and the modern state's minions; the education system, the various governmental ministries, the civil service, and the military. This is not to say that the effects of the presence of such sets of institutions might not be personally felt by individuals, it is merely to state that the institutions themselves can never be thought of as either personal or private.

The so-called 'private sector' remains public and impersonal no matter whether or not the state invests in it, and indeed in our time, most such organizations are 'public/private' hybrids, leading to a host of other conflicts, the most scandalous of which in any democracy is the two-tiered education system. In any case, the impersonal now appears to be larger than life, if such is only defined biographically or from the perspective of a smaller community of shared interest and action.

For Weber, modern rational organizations were anonymous, both in that very sense of 'being impersonal' and in their freedom from individual suasion and thus also obligation. Such an institution was part of his 'ideal types' analysis, which at first proclaims an ultimate arbitration but wherein reality absolute values were shunned and in fact finite goals structured all action. The very notion of the 'act', as both historical and visionary, the one providing a kind of testament to the other's cosmogonical birth, could not be part of any rationally self-defining organization, whether 'public' or 'private' sector. Just so, the modern rational individual - who is both private and public and participates almost equally in both self-defining 'sectors' in the more base sense of where the money comes from and who has sanctioned access to it – finds herself possessed by finite goals and is placed at a fair distance from any vision of an absolute value. Peter Berger, following upon Weber, has reiterated that what used to be understood as cosmic in both scope and import has oddly become what is most intimate and personal for us today; the religious vision is perhaps only the most obvious example of this transfiguration of ideals. Today, one can hang one's hat upon a personalist religious sensibility and this makes one all the *more* unique, the singular soldier of a Christianity that is about *your* soul and no other, for instance. In no other historically known period could this make any sense.

Similarly, the impersonality of modern institutions, however they may depart from Weber's ideal rationality and impunity from private interest, declaim their symbolic frontages as capable only within the realm of the cultural imaginary. That is, a state governs a people only insofar as it can convince the latter that it does not truly exist without them. In reality, modern government appears to exist in precisely this fashion, giving those who labor within it, elected or hired or appointed, the equally distanciated sense that though they are 'public servants', neither such a public, nor hence their service to it, in actuality exists.

So if we take the personal to be the space wherein action is contemplated in the privacy of one's own individual musings, wherein 'projects of action' are worked out in a speculative, 'phantasmatic' fashion, and within which one can decline any real social responsibility – thoughts are yet 'free', as is said – at once we must deny the activist's ideal. Instead, the personal is not necessarily, not yet, or yet never, the political. But we have seen it is otherwise with the impersonal. Though it strives, in its most rational and ideal form, to be apolitical, in reality and in history it is ever cleaving to this or that politics of the day. This is especially the case in nations where the civil service occupies a great proportion of institutional roles, such as in education or governmentality or health care. Only in the judiciary may we expect a strenuous public disavowal of the political, even though, once again, we know that the laws of today and indeed, on the ground, *how* any such set of laws is actually enforced and upon whom, are very much political in their origin.

What advantage does this discussion hold out for the individual who, on the one hand, must balance her private selfhood, her desires, her anxieties, her prostrate fears and visionary hopes, with her public persona and its singular ambitions, collective responsibilities, reciprocal obligations and loyalist duties, and on the other hand, that same person's efforts to translate thought into action without ever the sense that such ensuing action be either complete or yet completely fulfilled in its intended meaning? I think first of all that a clarification of what is meant by the term 'personal' is to our advantage. One, we no longer need guard it with such stentorian status; the personal is mostly just that, undeserving of much consideration from others, and so mutable as to dislocate our too-pious loyalty thereto. At the same time, two, the impersonal is laid more open to a general critique, some of which must emanate from a personalist perspective – in that I am affected sometimes intimately by anonymous actions originating in impersonal spaces; the stock market is perhaps the most obvious but also most egregious day-to-day example – and the remainder of which must hail from the hallows of history and as well advance from the actions of the culture at large. Three, if there is a dialectic at hand, it can only be envisioned not as some 'life/work balance', some other 'financial freedom', or yet an 'holistic health', to name a few casual catchphrases which likely construe a vulgar politics of their own. No, such an apex, such a synthesis, will only be achieved through the constant and consistent critical stance applied by an effective ethical consciousness that in itself has already understood itself as being neither personal nor political but rather historical through and through. For history is the answer to morality, the saboteur of ideology, the humanity in the organization, the humaneness in the individual. We are in our essence nothing other than historical beings, and our local divisions, our divided selfhoods, are within it once again united in concert within its deontological embrace.

The Question of Democracy

It is commonplace at the moment to point to the war in Ukraine as a test of democracy. Its meaning there, on the ground, is transparent enough. Belarus, essentially a 'client' state of Moscow, is a case in point regarding the potential shift in social freedoms that a defeated Ukraine might well undergo. But it is also the case that in general, most citizens in every nation want a society that is more free than it currently is. This is not to say that they simply desire to ape any specific other country, say Finland, which perennially tops the best countries' lists both in the objective scales of the world social health index and the more subjective sensibilities represented in the world happiness report, recently published for 2021. The idea of 'the best' aside for the moment, it remains clear that most 'average' citizens are yet vehicles for their respective traditions and thus do not entirely relish living in autocratic states. From Iran to North Korea, from Sudan to China and back again, what they do is make do.

The politics of autocracy differ from the cultures of tradition along a number of lines. One, State and Tradition hail from different historical worldviews. Where tradition has not, or has not yet, given way to ideology, its contents may be millennia old. Theocracies attempt to funnel some of these pre-modern or even ancient contents into their ideological platforms but the effect, though very real in some of its consequences – the 'Sharia' law in Iran, for instance – is yet symbolically fragile.

Modernity and its predecessors have never mixed well, and it is almost always the case that those who are attracted to the latter day sainthood of revivalism or yet millennialism are themselves from the social margins. Two, the State is originally an urban phenomena that is acquisitive; it needs to grow its franchise and thus its power in order to survive. Tradition tends to be rural and seeks only its own reproduction over ensuing generations. This second schism between politics and culture sees the State often 'dragging' traditionalists into what passes for the distended present, but this tension also prevents the State from looking too far ahead of itself. Fittingly, and lastly, tradition looks rearward and the State looks forward, though only to a point. This third difference is the most disturbing for anyone hoping for a better human future, or perhaps any human future at all.

It is a difficult mélange, our contemporary political culture. Democracies, limited as they are in reference even to their own ideals, struggle to balance competing interests yes, but more so, and more deeply, conflicting *claims* regarding the definition of the 'good' society. For the margins, the premise of an extant God may still be at work, fronting a promise that *any* future means the end of history and the transfiguration of humanity. Or, at least, some elect community thereof. These citizens have no authentic interest in democracy just as they may shun autocracy. Their path is toward an inner light. The problem they present to the rest of us is that their mission often seeks to include those who it patently resents, even if it is to merely bid us onward along the highway to hell. A significant minority of North Americans cleave to such traditions, no matter how Barnumesque they became over the course of the nineteenth century, and no matter how personalist became their 'beliefs'. In the crisis of today's democracy, it is equally important to look critically and candidly at the aspects of our own society that are fundamentally anti-democratic.

And it is easy enough to do so, even if the stakes seem lesser than on the battlefield afar. Our own conflicts of culture and politics center around the difference between premodern moralities and contemporary ethics. The first posits timeless principles, such as the Decalogue. The second searches for a new Decalogue, a different table of values that reflects a radically altered reality. But though we might be smug to the point of disdain should some old-world voice sermonize at us, the neo-conservative margins of liberal society serve us more as a convenient decoy; a way in which to transfer the burden of defending democracy as over against a straw person; someone who can be mocked, derided as if he were not actually present, not unlike our conception of the God who is supposedly dead and yet who maintains vast legions of faithful. Instead of allowing such self-made decoys to distract us, the authentic task placed in front of the true democrat is rather to examine one's own loyalties.

Three anti-democratic features immediately leap out from fully modern society, institutions that borrow only the trappings of traditions and those mostly as a marketing device. One, the presence of independent schools in our education system, two, the lack of proportional representation in our political system, and three, the prejudice against youth participating in that same system. The three are linked, of course. In order to lay more fully an authentic claim to actually *being* a democracy, all three must be rendered obsolete. First, all private, parochial, independent and charter schools in Canada must be shut down, their public funding – the reality that those who cannot afford to send their children to such schools nevertheless help pay for them through taxes is a scandal that approaches a kind of banal evil – redirected to a universal and singular school system. Such independent institutions serve only to reproduce status and wealth hierarchies and as such they are radically anti-democratic. The resources of the various elites – whether these are purely economic, as they are in most cases, or whether exclusion is practiced by ethnic background or religious creed – must be placed into the common pool. *This is how a democracy learns.* Second, proportional representation must be adopted at all political levels, replacing the so-called 'first-past-the-post' rubric. This will ensure that regional and local voices are heard in a manner that more reflects their diversity. *This is how a democracy governs.* Third, the voting age must be lowered to age twelve, reflecting the age already identified in Canadian law that separates childhood from youth. Persons of this age already can have sex with one another, cannot be physically coerced, can seek out health and wellness counsel, and are subject to legal penalties for transgressing the law. They are thus already judged to be fully human enough to also be able to vote, and are certainly cognitively capable of understanding 'the issues' as well as most average voters. It is another scandal tending towards evil that the same 'arguments' against youth voting were used to prevent women from voting. The very same. Consign such bigotry to the dustbin of the past. *This is how a democracy includes.*

One education system in which an atheist student can study Islam, and a Muslim student can study Buddhism, in which any student can learn Mandarin or a once this-gender student can transform themselves into that-gender and so on. And an expanded and far more representative political dynamic that will force politicians to be more attentive and perhaps even responsible to *all* citizens no matter their age or their voting patterns. Such changes are not only necessary for the future of democracy, they are as well a transparent signal to autocracy that *this* is what we are defending; no longer are we going to be tolerant of our own incomplete project regarding human freedom, and no longer will we wanly wink at the inequities that stain our own relative freedom and signal the leaders of unfreedom that we too, after all, have their immoral backs.

Mississippi Metastasized

This July marks the twentieth anniversary of when I left Mississippi. Reading the odd news item emanating from this 'southernmost place on earth', seemingly little has changed during the interim. Indeed, what appears to be occurring is that the sentiments that animate the old world vices of this haunted landscape are spreading, popping up in places distant from their epicenter, behaviors behaving more like a cancer than a culture. Sentiments of race and gender division, sentiments of law and order at any price, sentiments that keep youth as children overlong and bring them to conformity through violence, and sentiments that speak not of a *class* society, an outcome of contemporary economics, but rather one of *caste*, a symptom of an ancient and archaic worldview.

And speaking of which, not just sentiments, but sentimentalities as well. The 'last myth' of the apocalypse and ensuing divine judgment provides a ready rationalization for all of the other blights that mark the social fabric and tear at the tapestry of both civility and civilization alike. For the person who shuns the future, his vice must be turned to virtue, and there is no more sure solvent to assuage any conscience of its doubt than a fervent, nay, fervid, loyalty to Barnumesque religiosity.

I witnessed, and I use the term advisedly, much of this fervor first hand, even intimately. It provided a rationalization for the worst excesses of human behavior. One young woman with whom I became intimate was the child of evangelical parents. She had been whipped regularly growing up, until she had turned eighteen. Any hint of resistance on her part would end yet more badly for her. She related a time when she had simply run and locked her bedroom door. Her father kicked the lock right through and assaulted her with renewed vigor and 'righteous' vehemence. Shockingly, upon visiting her parents house, that same door remained in place *and* in its shattered state, years after the woman had moved out. She even pressed into her parents bedroom and opened one of their dresser drawers. I recall her lips parting and her body quivering as she showed me the belt that yet rusticated in that drawer.

And this was common practice, and apparently remains so, throughout a wide swath of the United States. Nineteen states still allow physical punishment in the schools, and many school boards ignore the federal law that bans it for those eighteen and older given that many eighteen year olds are still high school students and thus subject to such assaults. All fifty states allow 'discipline', an evil euphemism which can placed along the same spectrum as 'concentration camps', in the home. Many American children are unsafe wherever they go. My friend's brother received far worse, she told me, simply because he was a boy. If you were wondering why our cousins to the south live in such a violent society, look no further than how they raise their children.

And the other side of this costly coin I also witnessed. The beauty pageants and 'talent shows' for young girls; and when I say young, think of 'child marriage' young and yet younger. My friend, who had also been entered throughout her childhood and teen years in these spectacles, and I sat through performance after performance of highly sexualized dance and burlesque routines accomplished by girls four years old and up. The combination of such lurid displays ensconced within the iron rods of 'discipline' and an otherwise Victorian prudery created an explosive tension between men and women who, even in marriage, lived separate lives.

This four-square social division, black and white, male and female, is threatened by the LGBTQ2 and BLM movements, so it can come as no surprise that these progressive showings are resisted with great force by all whose loyalty is to a past, partly real – slavery, sexual violence against children and youth – and partly fake – this is 'true Christianity', *Leave it to Beaver* is the familial ideal – that neo-conservatism in general hangs its Bowlers and Stetsons upon. And it is *this* 'past' that is spreading, given phoenix wings by the anti-abortion politics, the misogyny of Great Awakening sectarians, the school curriculum restrictions, the book banning parents; the list goes on.

And Americans are aware of this conflict, though they seem hamstrung by it, transfixed by their own inability to counter it. When I travelled across New England in a job search in 2002 my Mississippi license plates gave the locals an excuse to abuse me wherever I went. Seldom did I get a moment to explain that in fact I was Canadian and that I simply had gone south for a job. When I did, the Yankees responded with 'well, shame on you then'. I lost count of the number of times I was flipped off, and blacks in the Northeast looked at me with a mixture of fear and loathing. In Mississippi itself, they threw rocks at my car while I was driving past, spat at me from across the street. But as soon as they came to know where I was from, all of that changed in an instant. Black people, students and others both, were fascinated, astonished that someone like me should appear in their world. *All* were aware of its vices, its evils, and all were ashamed of them, and shamed by them.

I was never so relieved to leave it behind. And so I had thought, for two decades. But what I see all around me today is a regression, a recidivism that desires to compel all of us to heed a real-time Gilead of epic proportion and yet narrow vision. 'Even' in Canada, you ask? In turn, my three years in Mississippi tells me to tell *you* to resist, at all costs, this regression and all like them; Putin, the Taliban, anti-abortion, child 'discipline', fake religions. If not, we may well find ourselves wishing to turn back the clock to a time when such resistance was still relevant.

The Greatest Challenge: The Human Future

I can only share what I am. Perhaps I look like your abusive father, the would-be domestic divinity who knows nothing but monopolizes false authority, or your condescending teacher, a channel for the 'dark sarcasm' of the classroom, or the talking head politician whose only interest is to attain power and thence maintain it. I am not a beautiful seventeen-year-old in a bikini, though I rather wish I was, if for nothing else than more of you would listen to me. But if by some exotic existential sleight of hand I could appear before you, youthful, stunning, healthy and charismatic, my message to you would be the same.

Exactly the same; that is, the '*new* three r's'. For while I am manifestly none of the above, I am yet your ally, your comrade, your supporter and your resource. But what is a middle-aged white straight European philosopher doing on social media? What *is* his message to global youth? First of all, let me apologize for addressing the world in English alone. The language of commerce and science but neither thought nor art, it is the only fluency available to me, and that is my loss. But in any tongue, even the undead language of those whose historical accomplishments are disdained by fashion, the perennial cause for thinking is ever and always the same; the pursuit of truth, the fight for justice.

And it is just now that both of these essential aspects of our shared human birthright are most at risk. And it is you, the young people of the world, who are at present being enslaved to a gross conformity of both expectation and aspiration, to whom I appeal. In every moment, you are told what to do, how to think, where to act. Imagine a world where no one can think, not because thought itself is dead, nor its essential language, but because no one has learned how. It is mostly the fault of we adults, but as we shall see a little later on, I cannot exempt youth themselves from any critical commentary on the turning away from the human future. For that is precisely what we are collectively engaged in, most of the time, in the vast majority of things that we do in our lives.

In no institution or organization are young people aided in learning how to think for themselves. Such a program would run contrary to the basic character of these places, whether schools, churches, youth clubs, sports teams, summer camps. Even the university is focused upon preparing you only for the changing and fickle job market, for somehow, you will have to find a way to survive. Thought, apart from the practical utility of the day to day, seems a petty luxury, unaffordable and unattainable alike. And yet thought is the *only* key to the human future; thinking our way forward is the hallmark of humankind alone.

But all of this is mere backdrop. Today, I want to call you to action; resist, rethink, redo. *These* are the 'new three r's':

Resist: when confronted with any authoritarian demand, any command of fascism, disobey, refuse to cooperate in any way and at any time. Examples are physical and sexual abuse, 'punishment' or 'discipline'; emotional and psychological torture, manipulative adults, charming 'authority figures'; petty rules of conduct of all kinds, school dress codes, vocabulary censorship, enforced activities, organized sports and camps. Waste no effort following *any* adult who insists upon obedience based upon either unreason or a simple display of power. Confront authority with the truth of thought, speak into being the power of human reason.

Rethink: change the scene of your encounters with adults from their rules to dialogue. Do not fool yourself when an adult suggests finding a 'common ground', or working out a 'compromise'. Authentic dialogue pierces into the heart of the matter, without restraint in the face of, or respect for, what *has* been called the 'sacred'. The adult world consists of the use and abuse of power, and it is something each generation must wrest away from those previous, sometimes by force, though it is important to note within the middle term of this triune process, that peaceful protest has attained its goals a full quarter more times than has that violent, over the course of the past century. It would be a cowardly and irresponsible act on my part to call to arms world youth while I sit safely in my study.

Redo: what has *passed* for thinking in institutions, in systems, in government, is precisely what has lead us to the brink of world annihilation. What adults have done, what we *do, does not work*. No sane person would follow along blithely and blindly, respecting adults simply because they are older, fearing them simply because they are stronger, obeying them simply because it is easier in the short term to do so. No thinking person would be satisfied, in any way, by the process and progress of the adult world: poverty, climate change, warfare, injustice, child abuse and torture, false religion, extorted science. Need we repeat such a damning list? There has never been a more momentous time for a redo, but *only* youth can accomplish it; that is, only yourselves.

You may be surprised that this is also a personal request on my behalf. For a decade my wife and I lived round the corner, quite unknowingly and unwittingly, to a school wherein young people were allegedly tortured and abused on a daily basis in the name of a false God. Such a God as these adults imagined must have been a pedophile, a sadist, a child abuser. Not even a devil would engage in such things. We drove by this place most days, never giving it a glance. It was simply part of the neighborhood, simply another place of learning. But what was being learned, what was being taught, was a brutal fear of the world and of intimate adults alike. Violent beatings, of both girls and boys, 'conversion therapy', 'exorcisms', all forcibly and cruelly undertaken, all highly illegal in my country, occurring in my very own backyard. I am ashamed of myself for not knowing, for not helping, for not stopping such things. I am ashamed of my country for letting such domestic terrorism take place and over a period of decades. No penalty exists in my country for such inhumane acts; there *is* no more vile a crime than the ritual abuse and torture of children; for it, and for all those adults involved, teachers, administrators, and parents *all*, if true, the death penalty must be reconsidered.

The courage of these young people, now belatedly coming forward, represents an astounding role model for all of us, but particularly for yourselves, my audience today. Yes, courage unabated, will unbroken, bravery unadulterated and indeed, bereft of any 'adult' sense of what constitutes purpose and agency, for we have lost almost all understanding of both in our own narrow, apolitical lives. Think now of your station, your own situation; are you not also being systematically robbed of your shared human birthright? The loss of human reason, the only thing that clearly separates us from the animals, and by virtue of this unique consciousness, human thought, human thinking; *this* is what is at stake.

And yet all is not lost, for the simple fact that all bullies are ultimately cowards. They will break before you will and before your *will*; your resistance will stultify them, your rethinking will mystify them, your redoing will vanquish them along with the dust and dross of all unthinking myth. I urge you now, as a world collective, to begin this gifted task, to take up this ultimate challenge. And I do so not without another critical observation. Yes, think about your condition, and learn to recognize all the signs of fascism, of bullying, right down to the tone of voice adults use, for in even in their most gentle paternalism they are talking down to you, pretending that you are not human, that you do not have reason, that you cannot think. This is what we adults desire of you; obedience unquestioning, parroting the desires of the commercial world, placing all your energy into labor, into service, into sporting, into the State, and at the cost of love, of art, and most especially, of thought. And forgive me if I am thorough, if I as well remand the atheist for his stupidity equal to that of the evangelist, for his is a faith in nothing at all. It is true that we do not hear of atheists torturing children, but their zealotry, their blind belief that there *is* no God nor can there ever have *been* a God is mindful of the same on the other side, as it were, the side in which a God is indubitably present and always has been, no questions asked or even imagined.

And my thoroughness cannot stop there, for the other question I feel you must ask yourselves today is 'what am *I* doing to vouchsafe the human future?', 'what am *I* doing that has any real merit to it?'. Another list: playing video games, playing sports, watching social media – how about that? – shopping and flaunting the fetish of commodities in your 'hauls' – how do the penitential factory workers of the global poor gain by your obliviousness? – experimenting with drugs, engaging in petty spats with your school chums, with your gossiping enemies, with your opposing team members, with those who belong to different cliques or yet participate in different activities - *all* without merit - than those you yourself take up. Twenty scant minutes a week to protest environmental degradation, taken at lunchtime, adoring the darling of parents and teachers and even some politicians? How is *any* of this of merit? No, it is pathetic, and the more so, it is this *inaction* of youth that allows we adults to dismiss you. *You* are only the reason that *we* are currently in control; the youth who frivolously expends her endless energy and her timeless beauty in shallow unending cul-de-sacs of self-absorbed vanity.

So add to your resistance all that you imagine you do for yourself. No, the vast bulk of these 'personal time' activities take you as far away from the world's reality as do the formal and officious duties that school, family, and the State impose upon you; *just* as far away. They are but the illusions contrived by those adults who desire in *you* a patent self-*delusion*. In one stroke, make your new 'three r's' destroy both the institutional culture of violence against youth *and* your own soporifics that you have used to pretend that such violence isn't there, that you are not being brainwashed at every moment, that your human birthright is not being taken from you by force. Understand instead that the new mythology is nothing other than *demythology*. That the future must be freed from the dead weight of the past, and that only you can free it, and by first freeing yourselves.

I have no simple parables for you. I am not a messiah any more than I am a demon. Where a figure like Jesus took a paragraph to explain the 'good Samaritan', I have taken 5500 pages of fiction to provide a blueprint for a better human future. But the upshot of both is the same: *'go and do likewise'*. Young people of all nations unite; you have nothing to lose but the past, you have a future to win.

Part Two:
Some Scandals of Thinking

We are not our own Justice

Shortly before his death, I happened to ask my father why he had become such an inveterate fan of the Montreal Canadiens. His answer astonished me, as this was the first time he had spoken of it, not in all of the long past years of my childhood and youth when we religiously watched the Habs each Saturday evening. They had drafted him back in 1945. He never donned the famous jersey as the joyful, though also incomplete and sobered, hordes of young men were returning from Europe and the talent pool got big again very quickly. Not to say my father was not a very competent 'triple A' player who faced off against the likes of Gordie Howe. He last laced up his skates in his early seventies, not unlike Howe himself.

Now one doesn't fact-check one's own father nearing his death, if even such a thing could be checked. At this point one has earned the right to make certain claims, not that I have ever doubted this specific one. I make claims as well that hurt no one but myself perhaps – that I am Canada's third leading social philosopher and ethicist behind Charles Taylor and Henri Giroux; that I am the leading thinker of my generation; that my 5500 page epic saga 'Kristen-Seraphim' is *the* story for our times *and* if one believes, as I do, that Jeshua ben Pantera, Saul of Tarsus, Prince Gautama, and Mohammed were all *real* people and thus the accounts of them and by them cannot be referred to as merely 'stories', then my epic is nothing less than the greatest *story* ever told – and in that I am no different from anyone else. But stories or no, the case becomes much different when we begin to make claims for others on their behalf.

And the case becomes not so much different again but much uglier when these claims are intended not only to wound the other but to 'cancel' him entirely. And this is what is occurring today in a similar circumstance as my father's end-of-war experience. I wrote about the concept of justice in a democracy in my 2013 book, *We other Nazis: how you and I are still like them.* In it, I suggested that liberal societies were at risk for authoritarian gestures not so much from their governments but rather, and with a horrible irony, from their citizens. For in a democracy one of the cornerstones is freedom of expression with that of association as the material manifestation of this first freedom. And so, one might well use such a freedom to express an opinion that in our digital age could carry far more weight about it than it otherwise would, or should. The 'cancel culture' that has become fashionable in our days seeks to declare this or that person to be a non-entity because of some real or imagined error of judgement committed by said person, mimicking authoritarian regimes of the old Soviet Bloc, for instance. (Romania, in 1948, declared composer Nicolae Bretan to be a 'non-person', and this was one of thousands of such incidents emanating from such *governments* that we both quite rightly fear and despise). But the source of the error is not what is ultimately at stake, for even a crime is a singular event in a life, and in a sober light related to that which bathed the veterans returning from the revealed horrors of 1945 Europe, no ethical person would hold to the idea of 'one strike, yer out!'. Indeed, much of the ethical majesty of the three more recent Agrarian age religious systems, Buddhism, Christianity, and Islam, centers around forbearance or forgiveness, both of which seem sadly lacking in our present climes. It is almost as if certain citizens imagine that they really are 'without sin', and thus the stones that are cast can claim a kind of other-worldly righteousness. In fact, such stones are the primitive projectiles of mere self-righteousness, a base sensibility that has animated much of the history of authoritarian politics. And if we are at least used to politicians themselves masquerading as ethical beings – in a democracy, we can always get rid of them come next election and try again – then it is much more disconcerting that fellow citizens become rabidly righteous and more than this, seek to project this base and narrow righteousness into society at large. Politicians who leap on such 'immoral panics' should be far more than ashamed of themselves, especially when they themselves have amply demonstrated an utter disregard for professional and political ethics. Hitler himself knew how much Anti-Semitism existed in Europe; he didn't have to create it but merely exploited its lengthy historical presence. Today's 'leaders' are apt to do the same with what Max Scheler analyzed as *ressentiment*; malicious existential envy.

What then is the source of such envy? The very hype and glamor that surrounds those we imagine to be graced with god-like fortune. To be drafted by a legendary sports franchise, for example, to win the lottery, to be the one to whom millions flock in concert tours or film releases or yet even 'religious' revivals, God help us. All such hype tells us that these few people are the best of the best, are somehow worthier than we, and that we should *serve* them, even indirectly. And however embittered, begrudging, or not quite convinced we may be regarding such claims, we do. But the briefest glance at the recent history of tabloid media and more tells us that we are ever ready for any take-down, evidenced or no. That the once mighty fall and we in our *ressentiment* rejoice. This is a misinterpretation of second wave Agrarian era ethics, borne on the once revolutionary sense that the 'first shall be last'. Instead of understanding these novel ethics as a potent critique of caste-based social organizations – it is important to recall that our much vaunted Greece and Rome were populated by at least forty percent slaves, for instance – we have personalized them on two fronts; one, they are wielded as a weapon of mere opinion or taste; and two, they target *individuals* and *not* social systems. They are the very stuff of inauthenticity, and Jesus, for one, knew that when he cautioned the stone-casting crowd to engage in a little self-reflection. Today, our democratic legal systems mostly recognize this caution by saying to the offender that though there *has* been an error, your life is *not* over, nor should it be. Indeed, the entire point of learning from one's mistakes is to live on *as* a better human being, as a better citizen, as a better *person*.

Especially is this the case when the offender is young, barely an adult, committing an error that we would associate mostly with youth. But the self-righteous – who must have stoned themselves into some kind of unreflective stupor before picking up those same stones and directing them at others – would end such a person's life and livelihood before it ever began. And that a national leader should agree and foment such a stoning. And that we live, so we claim, in a democracy of means, motives, and to a certain extent, materials as well. To this the ethicist, the philosopher, whatever his rank and standing and whether such a thing means little or nothing which is generally the case, *must* stand up and retort resoundingly, *no* and *no* again. Petty Hitlers aside, we are *not* our own justice. If a crime has been committed and the penalty paid, adjudicated in a formal and legal manner, then that must be an end of it. If one disagrees then it is the *law* that must be altered and not the life. And aren't we fortunate to live in nations where such an alteration is so easily made, without need of revolution, civil war, the cavil and cant of politicians, the death camps. And who are those who would give up this good fortune? Ask yourself if you value your freedom of expression so little that you would use it as an unmerited weapon against those who have cast *themselves* down well before any stone has yet been thrown.

Sentiment and Sentimentality

> If we want to abandon our daydreams, we must look at the *other thing* these ornaments are hiding and put ourselves in a state of methodical doubt in regard to them. (Merleau-Ponty, 1955:225, italics the text's).

The third of William James' legendary set of Gifford Lectures is entitled 'The Reality of the Unseen'. In it, he reminds us that reality is matched in human consciousness by 'unreality', or at the very least, a set of realities is balanced by a similar set of unrealities. Such a term, 'unreal', during the *fin de siècle* period meant less the uncanny or surreal and more simply the sense that it lacked agreement and rationality. The first due to its generally unobservable character, the second due to its resistance to being subject to reason. Yet James did not find the idea of unreality to be in itself unreasonable or even unempirical. Regions of the brain, separated only by 'the filmiest of screens', were either occlusive in their contiguities or were yet unexplored in their potential. Mapping the brain, as Broca had accomplished in James' own time, was not the same thing as understanding exactly how these different regions managed their internal affairs. Consciousness itself was thus constructed by apparatuses and architectures unseen yet real.

The reaction to Enlightenment transparency, the ideas of the individual, of free will, of sovereignty of thought, and their belated early Victorian offspring, progress, democracy, positivism, feminism, shared one powerful leitmotif. Evolution moved through unseen means. Phenotypes could be observed – even in our own time, when the genome is itself observable, the dynamic between genes and environment as well as mutation, genetic drift and so on, are not to be directly 'seen' – as the outcomes of a process the reality of which eluded Darwin though not, of course, Mendel. Consciousness, now radically remade as a 'social product' in Marx and Engels 1846 work – not published until 1932, mind you – also contained, or was yet contained by, an unseen reality. When Janet first proposed the idea of the unconscious he did so quite unconsciously, if you will, with none of the glaring threat and radically primordial overtones of Freud's later reworking. Perhaps it is better to describe Janet's efforts as 'unself-conscious', as juxtaposed with Freud's and given the latter's deeply self-reflective and philosophical construct. For our present purposes, however, we want to merely note that whether it is evolution, consciousness, empiricity as phenomenologically inclined, or structuralism in linguistics and later the social sciences, it is the 'reality of the unseen' that dominates post-enlightenment discourses.

Now is this the *same* unseen as James had in mind? Not at all, or at least, not entirely. If the Enlightenment, in its brash rationalism and its common-sense empiricism, had made the old idea of unreality flee into the cultic or rustic mindsets alone, it ran the tables for only a scant three generations before it itself began to be displaced. Like any revolution, the old regime – in this case, of thought in general and not specifically politics, though these seismic shifts are related – while defeated and in flight, doubles back upon the victors. It does so not by a pure counteroffensive, but by altering its self-conception. The old must displace itself from its own customary sentiments in order to reappear, through the back door, as it were, in a new set of guises but with the same basic principle in hand. What the unseen was to the religious worldview, James' ultimate topic, became the unseen within that scientific. Science, that paragon of Enlightenment practice, its 'application' of both reason and observation as redefined and reminted by the eighteenth century becomes, by the end of the nineteenth, a fertile field of occlusive discourses. From organismic evolution to psychology to phenomenology to structuralism, the conception of the unseen, of 'unreality', ensconces itself perhaps even more deeply than it had ever found itself to be in religion alone. For after all, however mysterious was the invisible hand of the divine, all would ultimately be revealed to human consciousness. There would be, in truth, no truth untold.

Can one say the same for the unseen that animates many of our most profound conceptions of modernity? Certainly, the race has been on, following the Second World War, to both provide a 'grand unified theory' in cosmology but also a unity of scientific understanding – sometimes referred to as 'levels theory' – regarding all human and non-human existence. Pike's 1957 opus attests to the reach of such a sentiment; that science can only overtake its predecessors by explaining as much as did these older forms of thought. In a word, science must both become the *new* religion and the *end* of religion. And it would do so by finally uncovering the conception of the unseen within its own novel discourses.

Yet this sentiment is a self-conception. If religion had its primal mover in unreality, its symptom in the uncanny but with the foreknowledge that the hand of God was ultimately a canny one – 'everything happens for a reason' becomes the mantra of the believer; the phrase is itself at best trivially true but the acolyte transforms such 'reason' into a connected *plan* – then science has the same in the surreality of cosmological evolution. It is, to our sensibility, *just* as unbelievable that the entire known universe should be as a point of light, that for eons nothing but cosmic background radiation should exist, that no other explanation need be given for existence entire, as it was to believe that a superior being with unexplained provenience and the more so, origin, should have simply created existence out of inexistence. At some level of reflection one is bound to ask, 'what's the difference?'.

And yet there *is* a difference, stark, stolid, and still as stunning as it must have been in 1859 or would have been in 1846; and that is, science presents a cosmos that is non-teleological; *it has no final purpose*. This differs in as radical a manner as possible from the previous metaphysics, wherein a final goal was assumed. And while Hegel attempted to preserve the *telos* of history, of spirit, in his phenomenology – such a dynamic was also unseen in its primacy, one can note – by the 1840s this had been rejected by the entire swath of younger thinkers, from Mill to Marx to Martineau to Darwin himself. In art, the difference between Beethoven and Wagner might be cast along similar lines, the difference between Goethe and Dickens perhaps as well. But most importantly, it was the concept of evolution – in spite of its own ultimately unexplained origins; what sets the serial universe in motion? – that departed from the sentiment that existence entire should have a purpose beyond itself.

In this, we are confronted by the whole question of the difference between sentiment and sentimentality. The one is customary, assumed, *unseen*. It is part of the social stock of knowledge at hand and is a lynchpin of contents for any phenomenology of culture or even of consciousness 'itself'. But the second is contrived, fashionable, observable and indeed, desires itself to *be* observed at all times and in all places by as many as possible. Sentimentality is as much a flaneur as is sentiment retiring. The one lives to see and be seen, the other would die before giving up its unseen reality to either science or religion. With the overturning of *telos* as reason, sentimentality overtakes sentiment as the compelling force animating human consciousness in its self-refracting lens.

Travelling alongside the conception of nothingness, a concept aberrant like no other to Western consciousness, 'atelos' provides a perverse reassurance that our worst selves need not concern themselves with the final ends given impetus by our egregious acts. The world could end, yes, but by our own hand. *We* own the end, we ourselves *are* the end entire. Perverse, yes, but such a term hardly begins to describe such a sentimentality as this. While it is mostly the case that mere sentiment cannot provide for either human freedom or authentic being, let alone thought – the 'sacrifice of the intellect', another one of James' famous phrases, is demanded by *any* set of traditions, customs, doctrines or doxa, not only those religious in character – it is rarely the case that traditions alone provoke the apocalypse. In our fear that revealed religion might self-construct self-destruction for all, believers and non-believers alike, have we not stepped too far away from the equally customary *sensibility* that a culture must simply be reproduced at all costs? We have, in our Enlightenment liberation, excised divinity and its teleological children from our sentiments only to be faced with a gnawing sense that without ultimate purpose, meaning too disappears.

Does this then also suggest that meaningfulness is no longer extant at all, or is it only hidden from us, a final effect of the transfigured conception of the unseen in our new reality? Merleau-Ponty asks us to consider this 'other thing', this *otherness* that now can only *be* other to us by maintaining itself 'underneath the ornament' of none other than sentimentality. I want to suggest that meaning does not necessarily have to be hitched up to purpose, and that just because we now live within a non-teleological modernity and live through and by an ateological consciousness, this does not demand either the reality of the unseen or the sacrifice of the intellect. Indeed, reality is all the more meaningful if it has a depth which is at first occluded, and the intellect is all the more real if its meanings emanate from both a fully conscious sensibility and an equally real unconscious sensitivity. If anything, the liberation of human freedom of the will frees up not so much humanity as a whole – perhaps each one of us tends in her own direction on this point; we each of us are thrown upon the pathless landscape of the purposeless truth and this *is* the meaning of ultimate freedom – but rather the ability for meaning to come to its *own* fulfillment freed up from final purposes and ends alike.

Interview with Zach Borden

ZB: From talking to you before and knowing you personally, and I know that you are an author and that you write multiple books of the kind that tie it into what you're saying. You know, does living in an area like this give you any inspiration or any kind of content for your books? And what is the back story behind your contemporary writing?

GVL: I've been very fortunate. I hear a lot of stories about other writers who either go for long periods without being able to write, or they move to places where the place itself somehow inhibits their writing. I've always been very fortunate to be able to write anywhere I've lived. I've lived all over North America, The West Coast, Mississippi, Missouri, Saskatchewan, BC, now in the Maritimes. So West Coast, East Coast, middle of the continents, and Southeast. I've been able to write more or less in all of those places, sometimes more, sometimes less, depending on what else is going on, but in each place, I guess I wouldn't suggest that the inspiration is necessarily immediate and place dependent. I think what happens at least for me, is that experiences get sedimented over time. And I might be involved in writing a novel, for example, where I'm pulling from, not directly, but pulling from experiences or feelings or relationships or conversations that have happened over the past 20 to 25 years in different places.

And then they get mixed in together, which is one of the reasons why it becomes fiction. In any particular example, you have a whole bunch of things that might have been facts at one time and in one place, and then they get processed. Not only does memory fail one as it does for all people, memories are partial in, if you will, two senses. They're incomplete, and they're also biased. So that double sense of partiality in memory; one of the constructive things you can do with that - because it's often seen as a weakness, of course, both of those things; to be biased and to be incomplete could objectively be seen as weaknesses. So one of the constructive things that comes out of this double idea of partiality is fiction.

The ability to imagine what might have been, or what could have been given some other slightly different circumstances. I think that's a big kick these days with streaming series which are slightly alternate reality. I'm sure you've seen some of those where it's not quite our world, but it's very similar. A kind of kind of 'Twilight Zone', like the series 'Black Mirror' played on back where the scenarios were recognizable, but they were just a little bit off. And then that little bit of distance gives the writer, and in that case, the screenwriter, a chance to not only show off, but also use their imagination to think about 'how can I tell a story that makes sense and is recognizable with recognizable characters that if we were in their shoes, we might act the same way, or we at least have empathy for them and sympathy for them'.

And then to make that somehow riveting, that's definitely part of the challenge. But it's a great and very exciting challenge to be involved in. So I say this and I'm in some ways starting at the end of the story here, because I came to fiction very late in my professional career. I was a university administrator for some years and when that posting ended, I found that 90%

of my workload suddenly vanished! I think anybody who's in management, you know, who's listening understands that. And maybe has experienced that. Well, what was I to do with all this extra time? I'd been writing non-fiction for years. I think that I had published already 20 volumes by that point, all either scholarly or scholarly non-fiction things that very few people would read and there's no fault there.

So then I thought, well, what about trying fiction? And I was, again, very fortunate, for our writer in residence, at the liberal arts college was a famous Canadian novelist. I got to know him and he was, as I like to say, my first victim, if you will! So you know, I had this little novella, which was essentially a romance novella with an edge. I said, would you read this? And he said, oh, sure. You know, and I'm sure he must have thought it was kind of a big joke. This is someone who's won the Governor General's award multiple times. Right. Yeah. Which is not something that I ever expect to do. So he read it and sat down with me and, and opened up with this:

He said, 'I don't really know how to say this delicately, but it's quite a bit better than I thought it would be'. Well coming from him I just thought this is a great compliment, you know, obviously maybe somebody would've thought, 'well, a somewhat backhanded compliment', but even so I took it as a compliment which was how it was meant. I took it as a sense that, okay, maybe I can do this with some practice. So he gave me a three hour writing workshop, face to face. First to first person was very, very helpful. He told me what needed to be done, but he didn't tell me how to do it. He left that to me, which was a good combination too. And I think that Zach, you know, when you're in management, you yourself have a very similar style there; you're asking people on our team to do something, but you're not directing it right...

ZB: Down. Yeah. Directly telling them what to do specifically.

GVL: Yeah. And that's a nice touch and this fellow had this touch. I'm not naming him because I doubt that he would want to be associated with some of the things I've written since then. We write very, very different kinds of fiction. And I know that my early fiction certainly raised his eyebrows. So it's only fair to keep that relationship anonymous, more or less. Anyway, I got help from one of Canada's leading lights. I still feel very grateful for that. I was very fortunate and it just pushed me off in the right direction. And I guess I haven't looked back since so that's been great and that's how I came to it. And then when I finally decided to give up my academic career, because I was starting to really get into writing and Jennifer and I wanted to live somewhere differently. And I wanted to go back home for a while. The sense was that I was ready to do something big. And that's how Kristen-Seraphim began; when I got out to Vancouver Island and settled down by early 2017.

ZB: And could you just, once again though I know personally, but for the audience, could you describe what the Kristen-Seraphim Saga is?

GVL: Well, what it ended up becoming is a 5,500 page 11 volume adventure epic! So it became, you know, a huge project. But again I was lucky enough to be able to follow that narrative, expand it and become intrigued by it, interested in it and playing with it, that it was for the most part a lot of fun to write and it didn't take all that long to push through it. So now, talking with you today at the end of June in 2021, that's been some years now since the final volume was even written. I think it's been over two years ago that that was now finished. And then there was a gap between - originally it was 10 volumes - that's the sort of canonical cycle...

And then I did a little trick that I associate with the science fiction writer. The famous American author Isaac Asimov, who would do follow-up novels set sometime later, just to revisit the scene. And my follow-up novel was set only 10 years later, not 10,000 years later! Which you sometimes find with true sci-fi. But it's the same thing, sort of the follow-up piece. And that was volume 11. So I don't know if there's gonna be any more. I do have a sketch for a 12th volume. I do have a title and I have a theme, but I haven't attempted to keep going with that. But it's a good point. It's a good time. You know, we may revisit this in some other conversation we have in the future. And I hope we do, but this is a good time to thank both you and Avi publicly for being so interested and generous with Kristen-Seraphim and everything that it represents for young people especially, but also for our company Vigilance Digital Media. So yeah, that work continues in a different way now.

ZB: Yeah! And I mean, first of all, thank you very much. But second of all, Greg, you guys pulling me on for Vigilance has been a dream come true. Since I was a kid this is what I want to do. This is! So if we can get this on our feet we're into the thick of it. It's a dream come true, honestly. So I appreciate you guys reaching out to me and pulling me on. But, I am curious, you know, as to why switch from creating your books and being an author to wanting to create digital products and create video games?

GVL: Well, of course I never imagined myself doing such a thing. I've already given away how far back I go. So it's no shame now to say that I cut my teeth on the Atari 2600 cartridge console playing 'Defender' and whatever other things, 'War Lords' and 'Video Olympics', which, as you know, used to be called 'pong sports', for lack of a better name. Very primitive games, but at the time, they could be quite transfixing, right? They could be quite involving. That was a couple of years when I was a very young person. Then I never went back to it. At the same time, I was aware of the Polish author's adventure cycle. It's kind of more of a Tolkien and medieval kind of cycle and in that it's completely different from Kristen-Seraphim, called 'The Witcher'.

And although these novels were written 25 to 30 years ago originally, they went through a process of translation and some small video game company in Poland picked them up, made a couple of games there, developed a cult following. And then when 'The Witcher Three' appeared, it kind of took that segment of the market by storm. It became a very famous game, made a lot of money, an incredible amount of money. Then the author realized that - because I think the author originally didn't think it was going to do anything - he recently received a 26 million USD settlement through the Polish government, ordering the company to pay him! We at Vigilance don't have that problem. We own all the copyright. The author is part of the team. We're not going to have any legal squabbles going forward.

But I was obviously a little bit astonished; for one, how many Polish speakers are there outside of Poland, right? Yeah, exactly. There can't be very many. So another big advantage Kristen-Seraphim had right out of the gates is that we're publishing in English. So there's that. And yet I saw that, okay, there's a precedent here. There's a precedent for getting, you know, a fairly bulky narrative into a digital format, reaching a much wider audience, and then that audience feeds back and says, oh, you know, 'maybe I should try reading the books'. They're very different from the games, but I think that that can be a good thing, a different experience. And of course that's one of the things that our team will have to decide: how closely is the digital narrative going to follow the canonical textual narrative?

And of course we can be as open about that as we feel we need to be. But that was what got me interested in thinking, 'okay, maybe I can do that'. Maybe we can do the same thing. We go from novels to games to streaming and perhaps even to film eventually. And so we're excited. I know that when I first met Avi he was really, really pleased to jump on and read the first three books very quickly, and then said to me, 'you know, I think we've got something here'. 'I think we've got something unique and powerful and it's never been done before'. And of course me coming into this industry, I wouldn't know. Right. And I've certainly had a very steep learning curve and I'm in your debt, Zach, as well as obviously for helping me along in this new world.

ZB: Yeah, no that's no problem.

GVL: I was just going to say it is a very different world. I mean I don't have too much experience in game development now, but with my little experience, it's not like any other industry that I know it; it's very demanding. It's very high pace. But at the same time, we have a lot of fun with it. I mean, I tell you all the time when we come into meetings, you know, that the team members were joking around or that we are kind of shooting the breeze and having fun, but like work is getting done at all times. And that's what I really appreciate about this industry. You know what I mean? Like, you can have a little bit of fun with it and you can carry on and get carried away, but it won't take away from the, the quality or the product.

ZB: No, presumably it will enhance it.

GVL: People like coming to work. I mean, that's one thing I've noticed. And certainly it's one thing that Avi as the chief of operations, has said, you know, we want to have a very different workplace culture in general versus other workplaces, no matter what sector, and then specifically versus the digital media sector. And I think that we're moving along really well with that. It's the kind of administrative post that I wish the universities could have imagined and I don't think that that kind of imagination is there, in any bureaucratic institution. So we're very lucky that way, too. But to really respond to your question directly, the first motivation for going digital was to sell books, you know, just to get people reading more, and to attract attention to the brand and attract attention to the ideas that are presented within these narratives.

ZB: To go back to when you were leaving your academic career. Was that just because that you wanted to be a writer or was there anything else that kind of pushed you out of being an educator?

GVL: There were a lot of things. As I grew older, well this is a bit of a platitude. But you know, I experienced it as a reality, as well as I grew older, the students grew younger and I found that there was an increasing disconnect between me and the students in the classroom. I found it more difficult to communicate, more difficult to interest them in existential themes and profound themes and historical themes. The level of literacy over 25 years, Zach, has dropped like a stone. Yeah. And I guess the industry that Vigilance is a part of is part of that story in a sense, in that the kinds of dialogue that I see scripted for your average video game, the literacy level is pretty low.

The conversations tend to be shallow. And mostly directive, because sometimes you're getting AI sequences telling you what you might need to do or what you might need to know. There's a technical side to it which is unavoidable in certain kinds of games. But the non-textual media in general, there's certainly a literacy. It has its own form of literacy; a kind of popular culture literacy or a game mechanics literacy. I'm very old school to that regard. I don't think that there's any substitute for reading. And by reading, I mean reading books, not the internet, not even newspapers, magazines, nothing like that. Yeah. Not even textbooks, which is almost what's left, if you go through a four year undergrad degree and you don't take an English class, right?

ZB: All you *do* read.

GVL: Textbooks. It's pretty much all textbooks. And that to me is also not reading.

ZB: No, I fully agree with you, Greg. I only recently came to this, and I was never a big reader and it was because, you know, school never got us to read. My teacher or my instructor always did the reading for us. So I actually became bad at reading as I got older. So I recently, within the last maybe two years, I was teaching myself to speed read because now I'm in a field where I constantly have to be learning and going through bits of documentation that are pages and pages long and this took me way too long because I was not a fast reader. So reading books has really, I mean, not even just improved my overall intellect, but just in general has improved a lot about me; the way I think of things, you know, I try be a little more optimistic because when you're reading books, it's usually from someone else's perspective. So you're gaining knowledge, but it's interesting. It's different.

You're right. It's very much different from a textbook and very much different from going to the internet or watching something on social media or a documentary. It is its own experience.

GVL: I think that this is a disconnect, and obviously I don't put this on the students there, these are young people, many of them straight out of high school, and you can't expect a lot of perspective. You certainly can't expect a lot of literacy. So this was my challenge and I took it up for some years, but over time it was just a period of diminishing returns. I felt like I didn't want to be in the classroom anymore. And as soon as, you know, a pedagogue feels this, as soon as I started feeling like I didn't want to be there, then I shouldn't be there. And it's that simple because I'm going in there and I'm not offering anything to people who need it the most, you know? I'm really in another place; in a word, I'm no longer doing my job as a pedagogue, as a teacher.

ZB: Well that can go both ways. You know, when a kid is not engaged in what they're learning, they won't show up. They'll physically show up, but they're not there mentally. They're not there to learn. And then, they might not even show up physically.

GVL: Yes. So in the end, you know, this lengthy management finished - I was in middle management and I was in executive management before that in the United States – and these posts always have a term to them. So when those terms came to an end, I started to write a little fiction and then I got this sense that maybe I could do that, from that novelist in question. And then I thought, I no longer want to be teaching in at least in the same way, in the same venue. And so that was a major factor too. There was a sense that Jennifer and I wanted to live in a different part of the country. We weren't happy where we were living.

Just in terms of region. I mean, nothing against the prairies. We met a lot of good people there and we still have friends from there. My dad was born in Saskatchewan. My mom was born in Winnipeg, so, you know, we're a very Western family. My sister was born in Calgary. My brother-in-law was born in Edmonton, so we have all of that funneling in. But I was born and raised on Vancouver Island and that's where I needed to be, or some version thereof which we've already talked about as well here. So that was also a variable. There was also a sense that I had done all I could within the university context as an educator and as a thinker. I had already been writing things that were much broader if you will, than any position that I held.

Some of the things that I was teaching were gravitating away and getting much broader and I hoped much, much deeper. And when you're looking to expand your audience, you can't write academic work, because it's because it's for specialists, right? You might have only a couple of dozen readers in the entire world who would even know what you're talking about. There's a severe limit then for that particular genre of writing and the only arena where that genre of writing is rewarded is the university. Okay. So you could stay there and just do that.

But I felt very strongly that I had more to say and I wanted to say it to ideally every living person. So the university was not a forum for that kind of work. I needed to get out in the world. I needed to, you know, so I'm sure some listeners will think, 'well, what he did was he just found reality'! He walked off the campus and as soon as he walked off the campus border, he discovered that there's a world out there. That is also a cliché, which is probably also half true. So like yourself picking up books and reading them, myself, just getting out into the world and living a more normal human life. Not only has it been very rich and innovating for writing fiction, it's also given me a lot of perspective on the non-fiction I write and it's made it better. It's definitely made my writing better. And the production; just having that full-time job, especially when I was in administration, the difference in what you can get done. Right, it's just the sheer difference in what you can do is astonishing to me. And I would never look back. I've never been in the classroom since then. It's been five and a half years. Since I've actually been inside a classroom of any kind, and I haven't lost a wink of sleep over it.

ZB: What subjects did you teach?

GVL: I started teaching in 1994, actually at Simon Fraser. And at the time our undergraduate program was the number one in the country. I think it's still, usually right up there with St. FX and some other like schools. And of course at that time I thought that this is my life. This is what I want to do. This is my dream job. And then I later became a professor when I moved to the United States. But I hold a PhD in the human sciences with a specialization in sociology and anthropology. And so I was teaching that for a long time. I taught in two criminology programs. Including teaching in addictions, which is certainly a topical thing, and health and illness, those kinds of things.

I later wrote a book in the health field, which I was never expecting to do. Way back I was also lucky enough to teach in the Great Books program in the United States, which is a national program that concentrates on literacy and reading kind of what are designated as canonical works in various historical periods from the ancient period, all the way to our own period. And that was some of the best classroom experience I've ever had, was teaching in the Great Books program. And I just loved that. You asked me about influences, why I start writing fiction. Well that goes way back, way back before I even imagined writing fiction,

I was teaching fiction for the first time. And I found that to be *such* an interesting experience, even in my own very amateurish, social science fashion.

I'm sure the Harvard literature professor would've sneered at what I was doing, but you know, it gave me a different angle. And if at the end of the day, somebody wanted to take an English class, well, go take an English class, right? There's nothing stopping you. So that was definitely an influence. I loved working in Great Books. And then when I came to Saskatoon teaching in sociology, teaching in religion, teaching social philosophy, and teaching in ethics and later aesthetics, it was an excellent position, a liberal arts position. I loved that. The scope was exactly what I needed, everything about the teaching position was fantastic. I'm still a huge unfailing supporter of liberal arts education. And I know that that is probably a fight that's already been fought and lost.

Sad to say. But that's part of my duty as a public intellectual, is to defend the liberal arts to defend the teaching of the *entire* history of human consciousness, not just the last 20 or 30 years of it, which we see a lot of that. And there's going to be viewers out there, Zach, who are gonna say, 'oh yeah, but he's just some old middle-aged bossy white guy who says that Aristotle said everything, and we don't need to read anything after Augustine'. And that's absolutely not what I'm saying. Right. I mean, it's like you approach any text in exactly the same way. You're a child of your time. You know, you might be 20 years old and it's 2020, and you're reading something from 2,500 years ago.

So how do you make that connection? In part that was my job to help young people make those connections, but also to help them understand that the world has changed radically. Radically, and many times, *and* it will change again. And so what we know today, we can understand ourselves much better by coming to terms with the fact that in every age people felt like they had just as good a self-understanding of themselves in their time as we do today. Just as good in every way, right? In explanation, in metaphysics, in the meaning of existence, in what the good life consisted of, in what made a good citizen or what was a good friendship, we can go back almost 3000 years in the West. And we can find responses to all of those questions in the same way that we can look at our own state and find responses; sometimes different ones, sometimes the same ones, for better or worse.

So we *are* connected, and this is why I have remained, even though I've been writing all over the place and also writing a lot of fiction, I remain more than supportive of the sense that if you want to learn something about yourself, then you've got an unprecedented amount of help at your fingertips. If you just learn how to access it. So from all the way back to whomever is writing today, from the pre-Socratics all the way to our own time, nothing left out. And I say that even though my education was hardly a classical education. I mean, I had a classics minor in my BA. I was lucky enough take a lot of classics courses in a very good program at the University of Victoria at the time. But I was working with colleagues who had degrees from Toronto, from American schools.

They had taken medieval studies, they were historians, or they were ancient scholars who knew and read Plato and Aristotle in the Greek! I was at an incredible disadvantage at one level. And yet this was a wonderful mix of a scholarly community where I could learn so much. I felt like I did learn a lot, probably not as much as I should have, could have, but I've learned a lot from my classical colleagues, my more traditional colleagues. I was always a humanist and I remain a humanist and so that's not to belabor it, but that's sort of my sense of just what's there. Just an incredible gift that human history has bequeathed to us. I mean, it's both a gift *and* a task, for we struggle under the weight of our own history of course.

But we also have this almost transcendental force in writing, in thinking in art, even in aspects of religion and in ethics that has also come down to us. Not come in complete form, of course, and not in unbiased form. If we go back to our double sense of the word 'partiality', history is partial in both those senses as well. It's incomplete. And it's biased. How do come to terms with both of those things, right? Do we seek to complete a history, and that seems like a vain and impossible task? Do we seek to make history unbiased? Well, how would we go about doing that when we ourselves are part of history, right? Clearly those are not the right responses. There's some other way to work with these challenges.

ZB: Yeah. Well, you know, I say it all the time. We tend to live in the past. It's good to learn about it, and it's good to understand why we shouldn't do the things that were done in the past, but even now I find a lot of people, even in my generation, they're fighting for some kind of racial cause or cultural cause that doesn't really affect them necessarily. It would affect someone that is in a different generation than them or that necessarily wasn't even a part of their family. For example, the Black Lives Matter movement. So me, being a black person, you know, the Black Lives Matter movement is big for me, but I live in Canada and currently it's the United States that is a mess right now.

So I couldn't go out and say, 'Hey, like, you know, the RCMP around here are harassing me because that's not true. It's false because I would see it on social media or I have saw it on social media or it has come up a couple of times. And now I think that I live in that reality when really I don't. And I know there's a lot of people out there that do that tend to do that. I say it all the time, we have to stop living in the past and start looking towards the future. It was my closing, my sign off for the first two videos of the 'Innovation Grid'.

GVL: Oh, that is the task of every living generation, is to not only live for its own future, but also to construct that future. The cliché of course is always that the future is an open book. Its pages are unwritten. We don't know when we turn the next page, what we're going to find and for a lot of people that creates, I think, an anxiety and indeed, we can go all the way back to the beginning of Western thought to identify what philosophers called the 'existential anxiety', right? And across the world, culture heroes of various stripes and creeds and genres have had this singular task if they have a human interest, as Prometheus did, as Raven on the Northwest coast did and does; to somehow bring light to the people, to their children, to their cousins, to these mortal animals which we are.

But one of the things that Western thought has imagined from the beginning that separates human consciousness from other known forms is that while we are aware that we have a finite existence, we're not going to live forever – and perhaps that will be changing fairly soon, I don't know – but at least for the moment and for human history, we've had the challenge of passing down what we've learned in a finite lifetime to those people who haven't had a chance to live and experience anything much yet. It's never been a simple task. I agree with you completely, that it's become a much more complex task than it's ever been. And there are many competing ideas of not only how to transmit knowledge, but as well what the definition of knowledge is in the first place.

So, you know, the challenges are many and manifold. And there's a sense that much cultural conflict within society at least, and perhaps also between societies, has to do with, 'well, *we* want the future to look like this'. And if you're not part of that, then, you know, you're not part of us! But the fact is that we are one species and one kind of consciousness on one planet. Thus far. And the future is *not* this *or* that. Right. The future is everything, and everything at once. So it's not a matter of making those kinds of choices. So then you have to talk about choices being made along ethnic lines or lines of creed, or perhaps socioeconomic indicator lines, class lines, vested interests of wealth versus the interests of the poor, the vested interests of the developing world versus the part of the world where wealth is concentrated. The tensions between rural and urban, the tensions between young and old. Okay. And, or younger and older, the tensions between and amongst the many genders and the many more genders that we're beginning to learn about as having existed and, and exist today. You know, this is in some ways old hat for the sociologist, because sociology has always said that gender is a performance. And it doesn't cleave to biological sex. There's nothing natural about it. If you will, it's something about the person themselves, it's highly individuated. And it can be shared like any belief system, but it's very fluid. I think one of the fashionable exclamations of people who are in anxiety about the future is that, 'oh my God, how many genders are there? I thought there were just two', and this was never the case. This might be scandalous to say, but I personally don't consider gender to be an interesting question because it's been something that's been around for ages. And ultimately one wonders if it wouldn't be better to get rid of the concept entirely.

ZB: That's what I was going to say; gender is just a construct. It's a label that someone else has created to identify someone's sexual orientation. So if it's becoming that, that label is the issue, it's just a label. We can remove it and everyone can still be an individual because yes, I am male and I identify as male, but someone else who identifies as male is going to be completely different in almost every aspect than me. So to me, I don't even like that argument. To me, gender is just a label and we don't even have to live by those labels, but at the same time, we're in a democracy where we do. So we're almost stuck between a rock and a hard place. So there has to be some kind of other option, we have to get rid of the label, or there's got to be some kind of other conclusion is what my opinion is. And that's just my opinion, of course.

GVL: Well, I've been told by authorities in human biology that even the concept of sex is hardly binary. There's something like five medical sexes, for example, including the hermaphrodite. So right from the get go, there's a sense that even a physiological marker has degrees, right? Let alone, as you say, a cultural construct, which is theoretically infinite in a sense, or at least indefinite. The sense of binarism, I mean, I don't know how far you want to go down that road, but the sense of binarism speaks to me about a kind of cultural anxiety more than anything else. In the same way that Freud and others have discussed the sense that we are abhorred by, or we're revolted by, the very thing that displeases us most within ourselves. So, when you hear people, for example, ranting against homosexuality or gay people or lesbians, my first thought is, oh well, *they're* gay. They just don't want to admit it. Or if a woman is unhappy with lesbians, then it's like, 'well, you know, that's because you *are* one and you're having trouble with your own self-understanding'.

ZB: Yeah! It's either some kind of self-conflict where it's almost a predisposition that they have. It's either that or their parents had a bias or their grandparents had a bias.

GVL: People feel maybe that they have to adhere to certain norms.

ZB: Once again, you know, social constructs, social norms, these are things that people have just created. And I find that we have conflicts over them all the time. And yet it's to me, just such a pointless thing to have a conflict over. Because once again, this is someone that someone else has created somewhere down the line and just said, 'Hey, you know, we're gonna start', first of all, if you really want to go all the way back language is just sounds that people have put a definition to, so, you know, even speaking English is just a bunch of random noises that you can understand.

GVL: They've become non-random over a long period of time, but I certainly take your point. You know, it was De Saussure in 1916, who certainly put it in an epigram and said 'the sign is arbitrary', right? This is sort of a famous principle of his and all he's getting at there is 'a rose by any other name'. There's a sense that in literature we have this sensibility that says, 'okay, well, what *is* in a name?' Shakespeare asks. And he doesn't directly answer it; a Shakespeare often doesn't answer his rhetorical questions directly. And that's a kind of a rhetorical trick. That a writer might use, especially a poet. But I think that we've been aware for a very long time about the arbitrariness of language.

There's a heated, really, an overheated popular debate regarding the use of what were plural pronouns for entities that appear to be singular beings. Beings like you and I, except they are plural to themselves. They and them. I think the thing that I would say, and this may sound very flippant, but I think the thing that I would say to people participating in that debate is simply that language changes over time. You know, let's not get excited about it in that way, because this is a function of human language and human communication is that it must change. To reflect the realities of the day. And it's been doing that as you say since day one, whenever that might have been.

ZB: Yeah. Well, that's what it comes down to. Right. You know, we've been talking a lot about the educational system and it's just these things evolve over time. And some of these systems or some of these ideologies that we have, have not evolved when they should. It's a very interesting thing because I tend to be optimistic and try and see both sides of it. It just takes me being optimistic to really be like, 'Hey, well, you know, why don't we change something without being too specific?' Of course, because I don't want, like you said, I don't want to dive down that road too, too much. So without being specific, I mean, when we talk about things going forward in the future, change is a very hard thing, but we have to evolve as humans. So I think people just need to learn to accept change a little bit better. And I know it's hard and that it's easier said than done, but it's something that is so crucial to the success for everyone.

GVL: Yeah. I mean, I think that we have to just simply remind ourselves that change will happen in any case, whether we want it or not, whether we like it or not. This is something that is our story as a human species. It is the story of human consciousness. It's the only constant, yet another platitude that is at least historically accurate; the only constant *is* change. And our relationship to change even in our personal lives can be very difficult. Certainly there are phases of life, which as you put it, are constructed very closely by social norms. There's a stage of childhood. There's a stage of youth. There's a stage of adulthood where one is on the up and up. There's a midlife that I'm experiencing now, which is in some ways that time of crisis that you are facing a mortality, which is much closer than you

129

might have been willing to acknowledge, and then you wonder, 'what can I do in the meanwhile, is it all downhill from here?' and all the rest of it, right?

If you have people my age and older running the world, what kind of future might you be able to expect just from that thing alone? You know, if you have a bunch of people who, like myself, are wondering about how much longer we have, what can we accomplish in the meantime, what is the meaning of what we have accomplished, if anything, and how do I start to die with a little bit of dignity and a little bit of grace? Those are the overwhelming, personal sensibilities of people my age and older. How then does that translate into political sensibilities? How does that translate into sensibilities that are supposed to be leading a much more diverse group of human beings? More diverse in age and gender, et cetera, to a shared future. When at a personal level we're starting to wind down and the future doesn't mean as much as it used to mean.

I think that that relationship is very real. I think that political decisions that are made by people who are Joe Biden's age or Xi's age, or Putin's age are colored by their own sense of who they are as a human being at the life stage they're in now. Someone might come up and say, 'well, you know, what should we do, put a 15 year old in the oval office and see what happens?'. I think some of the things that might come out of that might be actually quite good, but clearly there has to be some kind of balance between thinking that you yourself have a future that you and others your age obviously are in a stage of life where the future is everything. The past means nothing. But at my age, the balance is starting to tip the other way.

And this in that the past is starting to take on a greater weight. One is forced to confront one's past, in all of its potential iniquity, potential inequity. And then, you know, in confronting one's past, you think, 'well, this is the person I am now, how much of that other do I carry around with me? Where is it pushing me?' I think that that's a very real relationship in politics today, between politics and persons, because after all our world leaders are still like ourselves, they're still individual human beings. With all of the weaknesses and fragility that you and I share. With a lot more pressure than your average person, because everything falls on them. And there's not a lot of help out there for the Bidens and the Putins and the Xis of the world. Ultimately they have to make a decision and of then own that, in making that decision, whether it's the right one or not, or what's going to happen. The worst job in the world. They have to put up with.

ZB: I mean, that's why, for me personally, I'm not a huge fan of politics and it's hard for me to get into it because people talk like they know what they're doing when I'm like, 'well, if I was in that position, I'd have no clue what I'm doing'. So how does *he* know? Right.

GVL: And of course they don't.

ZB: And they take an educated guess, but they don't know a hundred percent and they're paid to portray like they do. And it just misleads people. One other thing I really don't like is the news. I think the news *is* just politics. It's not actual news. It doesn't actually project anything. Well, I can't say that it doesn't project stories that are very important, but usually they're projecting them with some political agenda, even if it's not overly apparent or even if it's not gonna sway anything in a drastic measure, it is still usually for some politic political gain.

GVL: No, there's an agenda to the news for sure. Perhaps ironically, it was Donald Trump who in some ways called attention to this, not for the purposes of reflective critique, no doubt. But at the same time it *was* correct to say, 'Hey, mainstream news is propaganda'. He never identified what kind of propaganda it was. Perhaps the so-called 'liberal' propaganda or 'secular' propaganda. Something that Americans would be more familiar with than Canadians. But the idea that an institution of media can slide sideways into being a tool for a certain kind of politics is something that I think we're very aware of now, in part thanks to Donald Trump. Again, ironically certainly, and also the sense that politicians can manipulate media to their own devices and certainly in countries that have a public broadcaster as does Canada.

Well, every time you turn the CBC on, you have to sort of hold your breath and say, 'okay, where is this coming from again?' And, is this Ottawa talking or is this Toronto talking, or does anybody know where and what this is? And who's paying the piper and all of those things? And is this where my tax money's gone this month and all the rest of it? I think that the so-called 'average' Canadian, whoever that person may be, is quite within their right to say, 'okay, I need to be cautious here. I need to be skeptical. I need to take a step back and say, what am I actually listening to?'

ZB: I think especially with social media, a lot of people just kind of really need to ask that question. You know, what am I listening to? I find a really big problem that we have is generalization, especially on social media. I've mentioned this a couple of times in my content, but it's when people say, they'll walk outside and once again, I'll use race, because I'm very familiar with race, but you know, they'll walk outside and they'll have one person or a select few individuals be derogatory or racial towards them. And they'll go on social media and angrily type out about white people in general. They'll just say 'white people were offensive to me today'. And everyone's like, 'whoa, you know, we gotta back up a little bit'. Like that's not how it is.

And we as humans do that a lot. I even catch myself doing it a lot and I try and stop myself every time that I do it. Especially on social media, because I made a reference last time to the 10th man room, which is the 10th man rule, excuse me: which is having 10 people in a room and you share an opinion or an idea. Usually one person is going to disagree and there could be more, there could be less, but like usually as a general rule, one person is going to disagree. But social media is 7.7 billion people standing in that room! So there's going to be a lot of people that disagree. So trying to be as specific as possible with your post or even with your language. Greg, I know you know this the most as an author being specific with your language, even in just an everyday post is very important because you read it one way, but someone is definitely going to read it another way and they could take offense to that or what have you…

How I Became Unemployable

I live in a city with two tales. One is a personal fiction, the other an impersonal reality. To say that I prefer the first is to dwell in the hermit's hut, safe from worldly fact and fancy alike. To recognize that the second is in fact wherein I actually live is to also, oddly, save myself from ignominy. For while the fiction allows me to imagine that I'm simply too good, or too bad, for said world, the reality saves me from blaming myself that I'm more simply the wrong person for the right job. Well, any job.

I was a professor for a quarter century. I taught at every level of the North American post-secondary system save that of the community college. I ended up at an R1 and as a department chair for five years. I won two university-wide teaching awards and was nominated for four others. I won over a hundred thousand dollars in publication awards. I made a comfortable six figures and had, in my opinion, the easiest job in the world. That others – many others – must have had the sense that being a professor was rather the narrowest job in that same world became apparent only when it was too late. For it turned out that when I decided I wanted to do something else with the remainder of my life I was warned vehemently against such rashness by my friends and colleagues.

I thought their cautions merely affectionate rather than realistically desperate. Surely I have many 'transferrable skills'? I have a lengthy résumé, I have years of executive management experience, more years of project management, and I had become an internationally recognized scholar in education, health, and aesthetics. What could possibly go wrong? My wife and I jumped the academic ship and our hurricane-resistant lifeboats immediately turned into flimsy life-rings. Over the next three years I applied to four hundred jobs, and my wife struggled to begin an entirely new career. It took her five years to succeed and in the meanwhile I got all of four interviews; one in a hundred. All I can say is 'thank god for PRIFs', as I never found another job of any kind. My wife is now a very successful senior financial advisor, so the once gendered tables have also been turned. The nub of the reality was that I had no recognizable skills. That careers are highly streamed. That an aging Gen-X'er has no role in the contemporary workplace.

But the fiction was what got me through to the other side of the reality. That it was my work as a philosopher that barred me from a public life of any kind. I was, in a word, a dangerous person. Anyone to whom nothing is sacred is, by definition, public enemy number one. Anyone whose vocation it is to critically examine society's most cherished possessions - its values - in another age might well have been burned. Anyone who bites off the very hand that provides safe succor to think at all deserves nothing at all from the cultural weald. My fifty-three books – thus far – qualify me for the dinosaur graveyard. Where's my OC? If Marc-Andre Hamelin has been dubbed a 'national treasure', then why not I? However phantasmagorical this other tale could become, it eventually allowed me to encounter, quite by chance, a growing group of young creative minds who, along with myself, started a private venture. I'm now the CEO and Creative Director of a video game software corporation and I enjoy it immensely. So you can keep your public policy jobs, your private consultants gigs, and your OCs to boot; this thinker and writer has gone radically digital in an age wherein the future is not plastics, but rather is as fluidly plastic as oneself must be in order to carry on in an ever-changing world. That, in the end, was the reality that the fiction was able to recreate.

Thinking in Systems

So you've graduated from high school. Some people call it the best years of your life, but you know better. It's time to step out, in fact, it's time for life to begin. Your life.

But dusting yourself off and walking out to greet the world is just the beginning. Nothing in school has really told you how to live. Yes, there were plenty of demands, but now they suddenly seem petty, things only a child would care about.

And then there's the big school, the university. Why should it be any different? Isn't it as well going to be filled with small demands according to it's own needs, and not *your* own? It speaks of offering something for everyone. That is, in an sense, what the term 'university' even means. It has the word universe inside it.

But if you go inside, where will you fit in? This is the first time no one's forcing you to be there, and no one knows who you are. This can be liberating, but it can also be alienating, mirroring the architecture of our wider society. And freedom is not so abstract as to allow you to simply live without doing anything at all. Some people say 'work to live' rather than 'live to work', but either way, you're going to have to make a choice.

And you won't have a lot of time to make it. Now that you're an adult, there's no more free rides. *If you can be anyone you want to be, the other side of that coin is that no one cares if you're anyone at all.*

So let's lay out the most common options that you are faced with, right up front: one, you could forget about the university entirely. Maybe it's just a bigger high school after all. And after high school, who'd want to take a chance that it isn't? But that means you have to find a job, and without anything more than a high school diploma, statistics tells us that over the life course, your career, if you get one, is going to stagnate. Even if you imagine yourself to be a born again pilgrim, *that* life isn't going to be easy, and might even be unfulfilling, lacking meaning. And two? Well, that requires a big commitment back into furthering your education. Most people find they can't do the kind of work necessary to get a Ph.D., so why bother at all? And forget about 'Dr. You', what about those stats that show that up to thirty percent of undergrad students drop out way before they've obtained even the lowest degree? And for those who *do* finish, the average degree completion time is over six years!

Neither of these options sounds promising. Many young people mix and match, working up to three part-time jobs just to pay for school. And then, if you *are* going to take the plunge, paying for it is just one challenge. *What*, exactly, are you going to be paying for?

It's a cliché that the parent will advise you to take a degree that will 'get you a job'. Anything else seems like a waste of time and money. But most jobs lack meaning, and most workers feel unfulfilled by them. How could it be, when you have your entire life ahead of you, that once *in* that life it often doesn't turn out the way you wanted? And older people will tell you that, sure. But when they do, it's not just a cautionary tale – don't let it happen to you! – no, there's something else in there, something born of bitterness and borne on resentment. It's another version of what in previous ages the older told the younger; I was beaten as a kid, it didn't do me any harm.

Well, fortunately, in most countries, no one can touch you these days, but even so, watch your back; there's a bigger whip on the horizon and its two-tailed: work in a low-status job for the rest of your life, compelled simply by having expenses and in so doing, accomplish nothing much; or get a bunch of degrees, if you can, and pay off your debt for much of that same life, working in better jobs but feeling just as compelled *to* work.

You might learn in philosophy class that communism, amongst other social ideas, promises an end to all of that. But starting a revolution is no easy business. Far too many of us benefit greatly from the system we have now, so why would we desire to alter it? No, you're going to have to learn how to 'think in systems'.

What we mean by that is also two-fold. Thinking isn't encouraged in our society, indeed, in any culture that we know of. At most, 'figuring things out' is acceptable, and only when such 'things are broke'. Now, this kind of practical reflection is indeed important. We wouldn't have come so far as human beings without it. But the one thing it doesn't do is help us adapt to change. In a word, we can't tell, by practical reflection alone, if something actually *is* broken or not.

So, one the one hand, a system is a way of thinking as it has always been. Sometimes this is called tradition, custom, 'what is done', 'the way things are', even and most brashly, 'human nature'. But history tells us that there is more than one human nature, and that such 'nature' that we might inhabit as human beings is subject to change. The question: 'can we change with it?' is one the entire world faces and faces together. Ask yourself right now how good a job you think we're doing with that?

But on the other hand, a system is also a manner in which *to* think; that is, I am going to think systematically about this or that. I'm *not* going to simply accept what has been, or what has been done, or even how it is done today, right now. Thinking systematically about a system of thought helps you dismantle it, piece by piece. You're going to find that revolution is not about politics after all, but rather simply, and much more accessibly, about human reason.

But you have to use it. Perhaps ironically, the university is the only place where this kind of thinking is allowed, and only in a very few kinds of courses. Fittingly, these types of courses will not help you get a 'good job'. Who reads philosophy? How many 'thinkers' does a society need? Why do people who think they know *how* to think, in turn think they can tell the rest of us *how* to live?

We're not telling you to become a professional philosopher. If you're already independently wealthy, then go for it, as long as you're also prepared for the ensuing facts that hardly anyone will listen to you and you will have very few friends. No, it is better to learn to think as a universal birthright of *who* you are: a human being. Reason is the chief characteristic that separates us from other animals. Human beings *can* think things through, whether it is fixing a machine or fixing the world. We are telling you to join us in the name of human reason, for that is the key to human freedom.

So, you might ask, this 'reason' thing, I think I like it, but how do I learn about it without killing my career chances? The simplest way to balance survival and meaning is take a shorter-term diploma or degree in an up-market field. Yes, the market for employment changes regularly, but usually not within the span of two to three years in specific regions. This is why more and more colleges and universities are offering theses kinds of programs. And within many of them, there is some space to take those *other* courses; you know, the spaces in which revolutions are born.

Bathing with Bach, Showering with Shostakovich

If one could choose a single word with which to describe our present day, let us suggest 'urgency'. We no longer live in a world wherein action has the time to evolve into act. A sense of the 'must' animates our every endeavor. This sense alone is, in itself, ancient, and likely begins in the eschatological time of Pauline anxiety, wherein the pilgrim finds himself concerned solely about whether the next is also the last. It might be a footstep forward into oblivion or salvation, it might be an action frozen into an act before its own history could be written. Urgency is a leitmotif in Western consciousness but until our post-war period, it has remained an abstraction; 'one knows not the moment', 'I will come like a thief in the night', and so on. This time of times is always put off; the end of the world is nigh but *what* end and *how* nigh?

Is it a simple matter of a reaction that, preceding the revolution of 1789 in France, the beginning of the modern age and the first herald that urgency was indeed coming down to earth, that for a century prior this same culture had been about a steady state of cultural celebration, with Louis XIV, the 'sun king', exhorting his artists to remember that he has bequeathed to them the highest of tasks, his *fame*, including of course his posterity. The highest of tasks was also thus the noblest of gifts. A Rousseau was possible within this stasis; his 'reveries' solitary and his walks perambulations which always returned to the center of things.

These are dreams without urgency, visions, hanging in the air above us, never touching the ground beneath. But a De Sade was impossible, for his nightmares, unleashed right at the moment of revolution, sound of nothing *but* urgencies, though they are base, vile, and sing the bass viol of the bowels of a now aged aristocratic chamber orchestra. These are nightmares without end, and thus even De Sade represents a transition in culture, and not the change once made. He is a liminal figure, which is one of the reasons his works remain, to a point, distressing. The orchestra is now staffed by chamber maids, even maidens, but it still sings of the domestic daily doings though shifted into the nocturnal.

Thus it remains within the contemplative life, which shuns action even for its own sake and makes all human interaction into an historical act before its time, before history has an opportunity to sabotage morality, and before the actors realize how petty are their desires, even in torture and murder. For Rousseau's Julie, a paragon of prudishness and propriety, is nevertheless the abstract ideal of the misogynist middle-ground. Nothing could be said against her even if equally nothing for her. But De Sade's Juliette is perverse, a heroine who forces us to reckon with our own desires ranged against her. Nothing can be said against her insofar as she in fact already has everything that we *want* her to possess. But unlike her predecessor, Juliette is also armed with all that can be said against *us*. She is an indictment of misogyny, and the fact that she enjoys being only this only makes us look the worse. If De Sade retained his liminality by never committing to social and political revolution but rather merely described the stultifying darkness of the Ancien Régime, his best and brightest heroine begins to sign the radical change that augurs the new desire. And she does so simply by virtue of her own desires being utterly *urgent*.

But these figures exist in a microcosm. What of the wider world-historical change that ushers in our own age and frames it at one end with the most solid of aesthetic and ethical foundations and at the other by nothing less than constant motion? This larger field, cast in the deepest relief in 1789, a centrifugal cauldron, a storm's eye, a nexus making cathexis, is still better represented by music than literature. At the far end towers yet the figure of Bach. He is summative, his art the result of a millennia of evolutionary architecture. His most important predecessor, Monteverdi, is Bach's own phylogenetic avatar. Here, and for the first time, Western music begins to assemble other forms, assimilate other sounds, throw upwards the folk song and pull downwards the religious chant. In Bach we at last have reached the zenith of everything the West represented to that time; the idea of the ideals, the mathematical symmetry of sound, the music of the spheres. And when the sun king dies in 1715, Bach's own star – and is it odd that Bach's face should so often be portrayed in our own time within a solar figure? – is about to ascend to heights no mere composer could have heretofore known. And this ascent is predicated, also for the first time, upon not patronage but upon art itself.

It is in the B Minor Mass that everything comes together. But this 'everything' is of course the *act*, never the action. It is the act against which all action must thenceforth take place and take its place. In this magnum opus, Bach presents the universe as it was known and knowable in his own day. It is a *statement* in the most stentorian terms. One bathes in such music; it does not wash over you but envelopes you, and while it is cleansing it retains the ability to magnify itself through one's very dross. When the work concludes, we do not feel any sense of change or that things *should* change in any way. We feel as *complete* as does the work itself. It is in this sense a space wherein life and death have been reconciled and no longer have any singular meaning. And how can we not be eternally grateful for such an expression of the cosmic force of existence uplifted into the essential?

But in fact that is the entire problem Bach poses for us. The 'eternal' character of gratitude is nothing but an obstacle to both evolution and to adaptation. It presumes upon a world itself unchanging, a cosmic order that is as infinite as it is timeless. Here, art does not imitate life but rather transcends it. This is the understanding that Bach, the divinely human architect, brings to the rest of us. This is the far side of the frame of modernity with which we still must reckon. It is *so* beautiful that it is like a death to turn away from it, and yet turn away we absolutely must.

In our own time we have, with halting harrow and tremulous trepidation, given ourselves the tools to do so. Beethoven is the first revolutionary composer. At first he imagined himself an ally of Napoleon, but after seeing the results of Austerlitz in Vienna, realized that he as an artist was the ambassador of the highest humanity and hardly the lowest. Thus the amended dedication of the third symphony, itself the first truly modern work of music. It is the first because for the first time we have a sense of the urgent throughout the work. Beethoven 3 is the benchmark for all such works that follow and the closest contemporary parallels to this work may be found in the symphonies of Shostakovich. They are linked by that singular sensibility, urgency, and tasked with that same singular ambition, revolution.

In Shostakovich we have found at last a role model untainted by politics and indeed, in his own life, as a prisoner of the Soviet State from time to time, as a suspect artist whose works were always too 'Western' for hardliners, as the musical equivalent of Solzhenitsyn and indeed more gifted, Shostakovich through his art not only defeated the evils of authoritarianism – it is an ongoing irony that his works are performed so often in today's

Russia – but also exposed the fraudulence of 1917. In Symphony 11, 'The Year 1905', we are thrust into *action*, not act! We are immersed in *urgency*, never somnolence! Many of his greatest works declare the pressing need for a *new* revolution, and not merely for Russia. His German counterpart, Hans Werner Henze, intoned the same: "Man's greatest work of art: world revolution."

Encountering Shostakovich one does not bathe, but rather showers. Here, even the water itself never stops moving. It takes the dross, without assimilation, down the drain of history with its own life ever onward. We are ourselves drained in such an encounter and this time the feeling is one of *incompleteness*. I am missing something, the music throws me forward. It is the future I am missing, the very human future, no longer a function of eschatology, no longer premised upon faith and promising salvation. No, in Shostakovich we receive a *demand* and not a promise. Revolution is ongoing just as history does not rest. Change is the only permanence, which sums our contradictory existence as active and acting beings who resist the future, the very thing that gives us life. Is it due only to an archaic sense of art that we flinch at the horizon? In contemporary art we find not beauty nor even transcendence, but rather the shadow work of the collective soul. Every encounter is a confrontation with ourselves, splayed open before the *Augenblick* of revolutionary lightning. If we turn away we are as were the Nazis, cowed into reactionary *diaboli* in the face of life as it now *is* and as it now must be. The fascist draws a line at the moment his conscience speaks. He will not hear it, not hear of it. Each one of us who adores Bach without reaching both hands out to the heroes of Shostakovich's works is no less that same fascist in spite of our apparent civility and 'good taste'.

For it is no matter of etiquette that animates the history of our own day. It is rather made meaningful through scruple, ethical and aesthetic at once. As John Berger suggested, we must vanquish the sense that great art carries humanity up and *over* its own condition in order to regain the sensibility that in fact what art *in reality* does is make *more* real our shared situation so that we in turn can more meaningfully negotiate it from within its midst. Art is and always will be our willing ally in any crisis. It is we who turn ourselves away from this joint task and reject its ever-revolutionary gift.

Anxiety and the Death Imagery of Desire

The mockery that death seeks to wield over life is no better exemplified than in the *risus sardonicus* that seems to betray its own irrationality at the thought of being able to taunt us from beyond the grave. Such a grinning gripping looking awry seems to say to us, 'here too is your fate, you'll see, and the thought of your realization of it makes me mirthful!' The immediate reaction of the living is to pretend that we have not seen such a face, to ignore its remorseless stare, as one looks away from the portrait that follows us too closely—especially if the ancestor had a notorious reputation—perhaps the looking awry threatens us with the same historical fate through a contagious magic or action at a distance—or perhaps the woman in the painting is not as pretty as we might desire, or the man not as handsome, etc. But the face of death appears in many guises, and we must constantly attempt to think of something other than its presence, the elephant in the room that is as inconvenient as it is immovable: "We don't know how to deal with death, and so we ignore it as much and for us as long as possible. We concentrate on life. The dying don't want to impose their plight on the people they love, even though they may be eager, even aching to talk about what it means now that they face it." (Taylor 2007:723). Yet this inability to 'deal with' is surely of recent origin, as all ethnographic work suggests that communities face death with an intimate solidarity. It is perhaps because we have lost this ability, at least culture-wide and in large-scale mass societies, that the inability to confront the head on the death's head shows up as an epiphenomenon. The rationalization of modern life has found its way even into the process of dying and beyond. Whether it is contrived and evil, as in the rationality of the gas-chambers, or individuated and existential—and once again, the figures of the Doctor and the Clinic are present at both extremes—there is a sense that the social fabric of modern organizations can aid us, can provide cover for us as we advance, haltingly, upon the horizons of our demise. Even our collective demise, which has the same kind of banal rationality about it as did the systematic genocides of our era, carries the logic of annihilation to its final step; a species-wide genocide that leaves no survivors of any kind. But this is too abstract, too much a part of the day to day in which we live, at least since the mid-1950s, to be of immanent concern. Rather, we stare back at the *risus sardonicus* mainly because we feel its stare to be a personal one—it is looking at us and no other. We begin to understand the authenticity of modernity when we notice this same gaze emanating from sources of rationality. When we return it, we enter into cultural critique. This desire to speak about death, even to Death itself, can aid us in speaking to the forces of suasion and centers of power that delimit our freedom whilst we are still alive. Indeed, this is the more important outcome of the desire to become intimate with death through dying: "Doctors and others fail to pick up on this desire, because they project their own reluctance to deal with death onto the patient." (ibid). There is also surely the banality of the profession that has its object human death, though not usually its goal. The Nazi Doctors were perhaps medically available to confuse the statuses of these two kinds of objects, and failed, miserably, to object to the second meaning of death as a result of a human process. In their collusion and their belief, they radically excerpted themselves from the empathy which the death of the other must awaken in us. But this distanciation is, in many lesser degrees, still a characteristic of all professionals who maintain their 'professionalism'. On the one hand, one could not survive oneself without doing some of this. The health worker would not last long if she became entwined with each patient. Too little empathy, on the other hand, and one also could not perform one's duty to the sick and dying. And this duty means not merely what is included in contractual obligations as a social role, health professional or otherwise. Duty here means, more importantly, the wider human and humane responsibility that each of us has to the other, because it is a self-responsibility that needs to occur as part of the process of self-understanding. The other, ideally, provides this self-same act and function for us, and not always directly in return.

Both because of such a duty, and in spite of it, the desire for death springs out of an ultimate desire for solitude and for a final adjudication of self-consciousness. For too long, we might imagine nearing the end of our mortality, have we been beholden to others. For too long have we put our existential needs in the background as we have looked to solve the problems of others, and indeed, somewhat more illusorily, the problem of otherness as a whole. Yet there is a final rite of passage that must be undertaken if we are to make authentic this desire for self-reliance in the in the face of death, and indeed, our impending demise aids us in doing so: "This dependence on other people, this fear of being forced to be alone, puts Self-Conscious man at the mercy of other people, so that he is forced to laugh when they say laugh and weep when they say weep [ ]. But 'other people' cannot save us from death, and death forces us to face our solitude." (Mendel 1974:217). The introspective desire for both the time and the being of a life lived, well or otherwise in our own valuation, is part of the character of this force. So the suasion of death is not at all about its dark mystery, but has everything to do with how one *has* lived, how one has run along toward it, which is why we have such idioms as 'running a good race', 'riding a good ride', and such-like in casual language.

That there are highly rationalized ways of meeting the death's head speak not only to our desire—'let's just get it over with, after all'—but as well rehearse the problem of being other-directed and reliant at the very moment when self-responsibility as the way to self-understanding is of the utmost. Of course, rehearsals can easily turn real, and indeed, specific rationalities plan to make them more authentic at the drop of a proverbial hat. *These* kinds of stages, set as they are not only by others but by abstract otherness such as the state, contrive to push us along into the face of death both prematurely and unethically. There is hardly time and space needed for reflection on the battlefield, or within the other extremes of wage-slavery. Speaking of the history of Tibet, Bataille notes something that can easily be generalized to any thinking people: "The creation of an army may have been rationally called for, but it was nonetheless at odds with the feeling upon which life was founded [but] To go back on so absolute a decision would have been to renounce oneself: it would have been like drowning to escape the rain." (op. cit. 106). The call to arms taken in a social context devoted to the preservation of life has a cunning about it that is not easily outlasted. 'We must defend ourselves', our *way* of life, we might say to ourselves, or at least, make a big show of it so the other thinks twice before attacking us. In doing so, however, the way of life itself has been transformed into the way of death, and this eventuality merely shows that the two of them do not ever really part ways in the first place. What we produce, the life of our culture is certainly merely one variant of the theme of humanity.

At the same time, our production does not occur in a void. When we make ourselves, we tend to unmake others, or at least, suggest that they remake themselves differently than they had done so before the wild-fire spread of capital and its attendant practices around the globe. Blackburn shows agreement with Bataille on this point, for "The true contrary to the concept of production, as of creation, however, is not that of consumption, but that of destruction. Consumption is merely a peculiarly creative form of destruction..." (Blackburn op. cit. 15). Indeed, it may not be as creative as all that, when we consider what we routinely consume and how we consume—vast hoards of persons gorging themselves with foodstuffs lacking in basic nutrients; vast hoards of the same and of others passively staring at images on screens small and large, and so on—these compulsions of the desire for death, since they attempt to enact an early death of both body and mind, organism and intellect, are also badly managed dress rehearsals for our ultimate, and sometimes collective, demise.

Such activities are the vulgar prosthetics of a promethean godhead that, in its mortal form, misunderstands the nature of the logos and of our relationship with historical Being in general. For some, the godhead that is also human, and thus imparts, at least analogically, the semi-divine abilities to destroy oneself piece by piece, is monstrous both in form and in principle: "It is strange and, at least to me, somewhat frightening to see with what enthusiasm many intellectuals embrace this monster, regarding it as a first step towards a 'more sublime' interpretation of divinity. On the other hand, the attitude is also very understandable for the remaining human features are features many intellectuals would love to possess...". (Feyerabend op. cit. 95). Why have the perverse patience for the gradual self-destruction of what is merely human, when one can imagine oneself as the relative omniscient to all other forms of known life, and thus give oneself the powers of ultimate and sudden destruction. We have given ourselves these powers, and their denouement is simply the wretched agony of the half-human animals who survive the first god-like strike. Along with this is the grim-faced dogmatism that all should respect our power, or our godhead. All will perish by the fire that is both vengeance and purification. Indeed, since there is a next world, and that a better one, all should welcome their sudden deaths and thus be converted, in the end, by the end.

The apocalypse as imagined by specific Western agrarian religions is of this kind, but it is ultimately only an hypostatization, an expression of human power writ into the world at large, an extension of the promethean power which was once the domain of authentic gods. Its dissemination to humanity was the most risky thing a higher being could do, because mortality knows best its own self, and thus its imagination is limited to the horizontal visions of the life-cycle, rather than the vantage point of the divine aerie. And so it takes revenge against itself whilst claiming liberation: "We would like to be able to concentrate all chemical action into a handful of gunpowder, all hatred into one swift poison, an immense and unutterable love into a humble gift. In the unconscious of a prescientific mind, fire does perform actions of this kind; an atom of fire in certain cosmological dreams is sufficient to set a whole world ablaze." (Bachelard, op. cit. 72). On the one hand there is such a desire that allays itself within the acts needed for day to day subsistence; the lighting and maintain of a fire, the cooking of animal flesh, the heating hearth of the domus, the sexual acts, the expressions of temper and argument, the social control of children, and what have you. But these are miniscule and routine activities, expressing as they do only what is deemed necessary, and not what is profound. We may embellish them in rituals, we may imagine that all humans must perform them regularly, but these luxuriant aspects of the simple life in fact make life worth living for, and not so much dying for, even if they do also make life not as simple as we might have expected. It remained to couple the desire for death with the unremitting love of life. These same apocalyptic religious ideas had within them the sense that through the end of the 'this-world', the other world would be brought about, or, at least brought into focus so that those who were once humans could now participate in such a realm. There was irony, but also, when forced upon others of all stripes, a sheer hypocrisy to any such movement that claimed salvation was at hand, but only through the allegory of destruction which, in retaining its metaphorical force—in conversion one is 'twice born', as it were—actually tells us that death is to be desired not for itself, but as a rite of ascension to eternal life: "...Christian doctrine and 'peace movements' may have had some deterrent effect on resort to violence, although it must be accepted against this view that the reality of the afterlife was evident and important to the true believer that it made death a less intimidating threat, even for its perpetrator, so long as penance and absolution were made." (Blackburn, op. cit. 130). One could, therefore, commit any violence in the name of both creation and destruction, because these two cosmic events had the same source, a godhead to which we are now trying to move toward. In doing so, we must repeat the acts of any God whose Being is the order of the universe as well as its moral suasion. In joining hands with such a force, we become as such a God is imagined to be, and it is perhaps this aspect of human desire that most equivocally translates our participation in the life-cycle of birth and death. That we can imagine such a cycle as eternal—witness the historically recent 'big bang' theory of creation and destruction which differs little from Eastern cosmogonies thousands of years old—is testament to the human desire to partake in the life-giving and life-ending events over and over again without end. It is a way of not only accepting our personal deaths, but death in general as the manner in which new life comes into the world and the cycle is continued. Indeed, the continuation of the cycle is what makes life worth dying for, for "...death distributes the passage of the generations over time. It constantly leaves the necessary room for the coming of the newborn, and we are wrong to curse *the one without whom we would not exist*. In reality, when we curse death we only fear ourselves. The severity of *our will* is what makes us tremble." (Bataille, op. cit. 34, italics the text's). If we are dishonest about our condition when we attempt to escape the 'luxuriance of life' in human form, as Bataille continues, it may be due to the sense that we experience the most intense form of the will to death, which will inevitably appear no matter how dishonest we may become in its face.

Indeed, we may be said to take ultimate pleasure only through the pain of leaving the human behind us, the path prepared before us by those we both love and hate—and even each of these we may have detracted or exonerated as the case may be, pending smaller contexts and interaction we may have experienced with them—and the privilege of seeing these people die before us. In the paroxysm of violence, lust and love become as one, and we drown our hatred of our own mortality in the desire to see the *will* of humanity come to a momentary end: "It is this paradox that defines surplus-enjoyment: it is not a surplus which simply attaches itself to some 'normal', fundamental enjoyment, because *enjoyment as such emerges only in this surplus*. If we subtract the surplus we lose enjoyment itself..." (Zizek, op. cit. 54, italics the text's). This *jouissance*, the focus of which is the extermination of desire through its final, fatal expression, codetermines the paradox of the human will to life, for it is what acts as the *Aufheben* of birth and death. Like the popular song 'Death by Sex', we must, upon entering into both the schematic and the experience of this surplus, be sure that we are both 'coming and going at the same time'. That the orgasm is referred to as the 'smaller death' in the stereotypically romantic language of the French only makes us laugh a little more, increasing our ability to enjoy this surplus of meaning by being a little sardonic about the allegory of union and the desired loss of oneself in and through the other, two exorbitantly flaming candles into one. Yes, the smirk of all 'well-laid' plans is the living expression of that later smile of rigor mortis, a smug complacency that one has died and yet lived to die another day.

Yet it is hardly only through pleasureful desire that we chase our own demise. There is an entirely different class of such experience that has been expressed as the dour abstinence from enjoyment, let alone joy: "Consider melancholy: black bile is not the cause of melancholy, it embodies it, it *is* melancholy. The emotional life is porous here again; it doesn't simply exist in an inner, mental space. Our vulnerability to the evil, the inwardly destructive, extends to more than just spirits which are malevolent. It goes beyond them to things which have now wills, but are nevertheless redolent with the evil meanings." (Taylor 2007:37). Whether or not one feels 'blue' or 'black' and so on has here to do with the presence or absence of an aspect of the wider world which is intrusively palpitating in its character. Even if such things are extant only in certain combinations of contexts— the body and the personality, the spirit and the place etc.—their force is one inherent to their character and this character is brought about by circumstances that have their own volition, but also within which we can participate. Taylor is correct to contrast the modern, clinical version of sadness or anomie, 'depression' or even ideational suicide as it is now referred to, but it is not merely the Cartesian division of ontological labor that is the source of this recent difference (cf. ibid). Rather, how one 'feels' about one's situation is also a thing in itself. Emotions have been shown to affect neural chemistry. It is an open debate as to which is the chicken and which the egg in these kinds of cases, and this ambiguity—indeed, the aleatory nature of these conditions is likely also near the root of their 'causality'; we cannot decide what is happening to us and thus as well how much we are responsible for our situation—itself ambiguates the distinction between mind and body. The clinician tells us we can control our own feelings; mind over matter. But the previous metaphysics gives similar advice: "If adversity hath killed his thousand, prosperity killed his ten thousand: therefore adversity is to be preferred; the one deceives, the other instructs: the one miserably happy, the other happily miserable: and therefore many Philosophers have voluntarily sought adversity, and so much commend it in their precepts." (Burton 1938:529 [1651]). This counsel suggests that the dictum *aspera ad astra* be taken as a directive; that is, only by going through adversity does one attain the heights (the stars) or immortality or eternity, etc. The interpretation, or at least the emphasis, changes by the time Beethoven takes over this phrase and makes it his motto. By the Romantic period, the dictum turns into a descriptive; that is, if you encounter adversity, keep going through it and you *will* attain the stars. This is the literary source of Churchill's optimistic and yet sardonic comment about 'going through hell'. But the major pivot upon which melancholy suffered its shift of meaning came through the attribution of *depth* to sorrow. This was also a Romantic leitmotif: "Sadness made one 'interesting'. It was the mark of refinement, of sensibility, to be sad. That is, to be powerless." (Sontag 1978:31). The one who seemingly voluntaristically turned away from the pursuit of power, and was also seen to give it up in one's personal affairs to the point of not being able to laugh, take a joke, or get out of bed in the morning, became a kind of fetish for the introspective intellect of the Romantics. The old quip about the famous novelist who ultimately ruined his career because he gave up alcoholism, nocturnal wanderings and depression is well taken here. By the time we react to this framework along the way to the encounter the psychoanalytic archaeology of the matter of sorrow's continuity and its mythological self-referencing to the fallen state of humanity, the abilities we have to work in the world have been cast as being attracted to the light, as it were, while the dangers of navel-gazing are attributed to self-interested thinking and the desire for death. At first, it is Hegel "...who argues that vision and hearing are the proper senses of art because all of the other senses are stimulated by the effects of a destruction of the world. Freud seems to agree with this argument..." (Horowitz 2001:228). Though Freud attributes the ascendance of such a worldly sense to evolutionary biology, organismic adaptation alone could not have produced the self-concept. Indeed, one would think altruism to be the more refined sensibility of an animal that had both volition and reflection, with or without the *sensus communis* of the social contract. Given this, "One is often tempted to wonder whether, if Freud had recognized the internal economy of melancholia *before* he formulated his theory of narcissism, he and Abraham would not themselves have carried further their exploration of intra-psychic animism." (Brierley 1951:81 italics the text's). The sense that the self can feed back into itself only self-directedness has a touch of the narcotic about it. Indeed, Brierley herself suggests the 'magical' quality of such a conception which surely is fitting given the problem a new and rational discourse of the irrational suggesting that such thinking only occurs *outside* the model of consciousness it proposes; that is, only as unreflected reactive thinking and doing which is sourced in the unconscious life: "Its exploration is of great importance, since the more irrational aspects of human life and behaviour, e.g. the sphere of beliefs and values, not to mention politics, are largely dominated by animistic thinking, and rational thinking is far more influenced by it than is generally recognized. The proportion of rationalization in reasoning is frequently high." (ibid). It is striking, and heartening, to note that a mid-twentieth century female critic was unafraid to state clearly the truth of the male-dominated public life as being ironically, and paradoxically, shot through with either irrational actions and non-rational value systems. The latter might even be seen to have become the former through the very process of rationalization in modern institutional life. Perhaps in the wake of Nuremberg it was more obvious that politics was so dominated, but it is a critique that we cannot afford to leave behind us.

Given that the 'interesting' quality of the person who has given himself over to sadness might well merge with the magical quality of the person who attempts to be charismatic in a rational/legal system of authority, the social role of such a person—perhaps an odd inversion of the village idiot in the realm of the intellectual or the political; a figure of projected pity turned into a figure of unholy fascination—introduces a convolution into the path of desire on its way to the place of death. We are distracted from the course through lingering with the potential malingerer. Yet in the meanwhile, the other end of the thread continues its motion. Death itself does not tarry awhile with the living dead. Soon enough our more authenticating desire tears us away from the way-stations of theater, the half-way houses of the morose or the charming, the smaller than life and the larger than life, their *gravis* unable to finish their own graves. And so we continue: "He approached death, which approached him, more and more quickly; he approached it in preceding it, and anticipated it with these images and glosses, for which the grammar of the future anterior no doubt does not suffice to convey their force and time, their sense." (Derrida 2001:157). The temporality of self-mourning, Derrida continues, does not give itself over to the language of prediction or predication. We might well add that working through mourning is the manner in which we allow ourselves to accept that we are not only moving along in the direction of our demise, but that death as an empirical event, and as no mere harbinger, is moving along that self-same path. We confront this situation as one that takes us outside of the closed loop of originary psycho-analytic melancholy, as its act appears to us as a 'sacrifice', "...a pure loss without any narcissistic benefit." (Zizek op. cit. 127). It is one that we hesitate to make in its entirety, at least at first, because the desire for death also wishes to keep on reproducing its desire. Hence its alteration and inverse perambulations in the wake of tragedy, the waking of sorrows, and the wakes held as social spaces of the reaffirmation of community. Such a desire has only itself to consume, but this is not ultimately a paradox: "This contradiction, at the very root of the intuition of being, favors endless transformations of value." (Bachelard, op. cit. 79). It is these translations, such as sorrow or contrived political charm, apocalyptic thinking at once waiting to be saved by the one who overcomes the apocalypse, madness ascending through reason, melancholia rescued by charisma—and how often do we imagine that the 'mentally ill' simply need someone to *love* them selflessly?—that give us the sense that "Since we must disappear, since the instinct for death will impose itself one day on the most exuberant life, let us disappear and die completely. Let us destroy the fire of our life by a superfire, by a superhuman superfire without flame or ashes, which will bring extinction to the very heart of the being." (ibid). This kind of destruction is not everything the heart alone desires, but rather is all mortality can do to itself to prove its own existence as a guise of Being. In immolating itself in a manner that no mortality could withstand, the desires of the heart are finally overcome.

It is not only the imagined subject that is the object of its own demise. The mortality of the object too cannot be objected to in too abject a way. What is destroyed by an 'inflammation' of Being, by the inflammatory language of the other, or yet further through the conflagration of transmigrating spirit, its ascent arrested in mid-air by a voice of flame speaking in the unknowable tongue of the dead, is more akin to an object in the object realm. In any case, it no longer 'lives' in the usual manner of living things. It has wasted itself upon living, as it were, and now must record how such a consumption of life was, after all, also a consummation of it. This has a special effect upon the human being as both an organism in a chain but also as the source of all authentic wastefulness in a nature from which he is partially exempt: "The general movement of exudation (of waste) of living matter impels him, and he cannot stop it; moreover, being at the summit. His sovereignty in the living world identifies him with this movement; it destines him, in a privileged way, to that glorious operation, to useless consumption." (Bataille, op. cit. 23). We may well criticize this kind of activity as being egoistic in the extreme. What right do we have, ask the few, to make the earth our garbage-scow, traversing the ellipse like a pariah barge, never nearing close enough to the ultimate fire to be consumed in an ultimate event? Yet we are also carrion-eaters, we consume our own garbage, so that the earth only slowly reveals its human transformation—greenhouse gases, irradiated lakes and the like—and in its inorganic non-conscious justice, becomes unlivable at the very point when humanity must be destroyed. In other words, the earth as a world of humans conceals its own *risus sardonicus* until it can flash the grin at us when it will mean the most. This time may well be fast approaching, but like our individual deaths, the point of no return is difficult to precisely predict. One will know it when it occurs, we are told, somewhat perversely, as if some Pauline environmentalist had come back from the Levantine birthplace of world-denying soteriology to announce the final denial of the world, though this time, with his own death-mask smirk, to then reveal no paradise to which we as a species might exeunt. So egotism revels at all corners of this predicament. It wastes exuberantly, while all the while it warns smugly. It desires to be both the deed and the doer, the criminal and the detective. It wants to possess for itself alone both the success of the crime and the accolade for its solution, except in this case the crime cannot be absolved by our collective perpetration being caught up in the folding nets of an imploding ecosphere. And rather than admitting to such deeds and thus then attempting to pay a remittance for them, committing to rehabilitate the damage we have done with a view to the future, we blame the ego in our subjectitude for seeking revenge against a world we imagine has tried to imprison it in the object. Thus the ego becomes a freedom-fighter who circumnavigates the child-self by claiming that it is 'too mature' to be distracted by the visions of the child, this latter wishing to conjure again the pristine garden of its birth. The ego, rather, imagines itself, and is imagined by an entire discourse, to be the source of a problem that only it can solve. It has given itself, quite egotistically, a sacred task, and yet the problem is that of the 'dirty job' which 'someone has to do': "It's the latest fetish introduced into the holy of holies of a practice that is legitimated by the superiority of the superiors. It does the job as well as any other, everyone realizing that it is always the most outmoded, dirty, and repulsive object that best fulfills this function—this function being entirely real." (Lacan 2004:124 [1966]). Once taken up, however, such a job quickly reveals itself as a drudge. No singularity of prideful or resourceful egotism could ever clean up its own act. This is where the excavation skills of a psychoanalysis appear on the scene, bearing with them their heavy equipment, discursive apparatuses that can dig the deepest hole. If this kind of operation fails, the gaping gap-toothed hole can at least be used to dump more garbage into, out of sight, and quite literally out of mind! Mouths agape, these forays into the structure of the self perhaps reveal more about our uncanny ability to distract ourselves from the pragmatic task of curbing our exuberance regarding consumption of resources and production of waste, in which we North Americans provide the Olympian epitomes. No surprise here, given that we live in the most highly individuated society in history, our egos striving for, more than anything else, an inequality of egotism. At the same time, there is also, as we have seen, a strong desire to be the savior, even to sacrifice our own life through the proclamation that our ego was the herald of continued life, that our vision was more realistic and forward-thinking than all others. In doing so, we allow ourselves to participate in yet another version of the smug smirk of death, this time combining melancholia and desire. In this, the human being "...*realizes* his discouragement and impotency; he makes a phantom of his own fatigue. Thus the mark of changeable man is placed upon things. That which diminishes or increases within ourselves becomes a sign of a life that is either stifled or fully awakened within reality." (Bachelard, op. cit. 45). Perhaps this is the most salient of all the errors which appeals to the half-objectified half-objected-to subjectivity of humanity. We desire most of all to make sure that our way of life is projected onto an objective landscape where it can remain unchanged. The pyramids of Giza may be the most obvious of examples, monuments to a mortality which are transfigured into an immortality that seeks to deny the history of beings. Even their presence in a desert, deserted of the usual foliage and organisms that enliven the stolid earth is of more than metaphoric interest. Or perhaps the landscape of the pyramids has become a desert over time, the energy and resources drawn up into the limestone edifices, like trees sucking water from their immediate hinterlands. Such an energy, we may imagine, performs some occult function in the process begun by the original practitioners of the greatest occult science, the priestly preservation of life through death.

Such monuments represent the will to have both an increase of being and an expression of desireful longing to become larger than life. Such a duet of options is, however, rarely in tune with itself: "If we have the choice between that which appeals to us and that which increases our resources, it is always hard to give up our desire in exchange for future benefits. It may be easy if we are in good condition: Rational interest operates without hindrance. But if we are exhausted, only terror and exaltation keep us from going slack." (Bataille, op. cit. 164-5). If the desire for nothingness merges the two, ultimate fear and joy now both operating them without limits, this must be the vivisection that produces the exhaust of auto-combustion. Yet we do not wish to die at the hands of just any worldly force. The sensibility that we must be the authors of our own demise also appears to be just as rational. This is so because only within our own hearths do we find that we no longer die alone, especially in the non-rational worldviews of pre-industrial social organizations, for it is within the hearth that we are recalled to our true community, the circle that gave us birth and nurtured us, both in the reality of place and in social reality. Of course, the sense that one cannot die a stranger to one's own land produced long-lasting biases against any form of otherness which in most regions of the world have lasted in a variety of sometimes little-altered forms to our own day. Nevertheless, "Fear of the alien, in particular the alien soldier, had a quite rational basis which helps explain the frequent manifestations of xenophobia and particularism that were characteristic of the pre-modern world." (Blackburn, op. cit. 62). If dying amongst one's community, within the interiority of the hypostasized self which itself gave life to our selves is the ideal, and remains so—one only need think of the hospital death and the home death to bring this sentiment to the forefront of our anxieties, the former too rationalized, the latter with just enough of the non-rational 'homey' quality to make it part of the magic circle of life—there are still instances where we are called upon to pass away the quietude of 'going in one's sleep' for the still romanticized heroism of 'dying with one's boots on'. If this is to be the case, there is another response that our community makes on our behalf. This is especially or ultimately so "...when the actions involved also imply, for the participants, the facing of an incalculably weighty risk—their own death—then ritualization, by freeing the mind from the need to ponder, is probably effective." (Gellner 1985:80). Ironically, the lack of forethought regarding the desire for self-immolation helps the process along to it's sought after conclusion. The feelings that hold us back have to do not with the loss of life, but of the anticipated lost, or at least, radically transformed, quality of love and community without which we would have never lived in the first place.

The hypostatization of death therefore involves us in its own circle, articulated through a rite of passage that has no identifiable terminus, at least from this side of the 'river'. Just as the boundary flows along with no apparent or visible stoppage, no place of rest, one must traverse this symbolic obstacle in order to do just that. 'Eternal rest;' it may not be, but exhaustion means that one *must* rest, for however lengthy a period, liminal, purgatorial, heavenly, and one of the great fears regarding the hellishness of all imagined underworlds where there is to be not an evaluatory sojourn but an indefinite or even an everlasting sentence is that there exists and can exist no rest nor hope of rest in these horrifying places. When we perish, exhausted by the flames of life, driven to death by the desire to live in the fullest possible manner, we also may well feel we have done such a job of it that rest is deserved. Certainly, archaic soteriologies of self-knowledge weigh this part of their other-worldly evaluation quite heavily. Was one's life well-lived, did one manufacture a *good* life, rather than merely *the* good life? Did one live on as a good human being rather than merely as a human being who lived well, high on the hog of neo-colonialism. When Aristotle reminds us that the 'best revenge is living well', he means both of these things to be intimately related: that the ethical life generates the 'good life' for itself. Otherwise, we become obsessed by a history that rematerializes in front of us at the slightest insult. We never overcome the thingness that we have let it become. We are becalmed in its waters, drifting ever closer to the ghostly derelict that we know, once close to, or yet more terrifyingly, once aboard, we are no longer our own masters and must succumb to *ressentiment* and further, neurosis. Therefore, the overcoming of the resented meanings through the forgetting of history which Nietzsche recommends, avoids the problem of pouring human meaningfulness into a void—or perverting it by producing the waste that fills in the holes in our consciousness, as above—and ameliorates the drive to "...attempt to domesticate the Thing by reducing it to its symbolic status, by providing it with a meaning. We usually say that the fascinating presence of a Thing obscures its meaning; here, we say the opposite is true: the meaning obscures the terrifying impact of its presence." (Zizek, op. cit. 77). The thingness of an object gone wild, broken out beyond our control—Zizek uses RMS Titanic, the most famous, though hardly the most horrifying, shipwreck of modernity to illustrate his point—produces its new Lovecraftian status of the Thing which should *not* have been. We should, we reiterate to ourselves and whoever else might *listen* to us, have been able to control things better: steer the ship, slow her down, post more lookouts, provide searchlights, take a different course, not listen to passenger's advice or hubris—it is amazing, looking at the history of modern shipwrecks, how often senior crewmen and deck officers give in to their passenger's desires (witness the very recent and ridiculous wreck of the Italian cruise ship MV Costa Concordia)—but in the end we did not. This 'end' indeed must produce the effect of losing control over things, of making them thus the Thing which overcomes our uncapitalized beings. We did not capitalize upon our existence when we needed to, or perhaps we knew this and deliberately desired to remain small in the face of a world rewriting itself as immanent before our very eyes. This is the fascination of which Zizek speaks, and to pretend to its non-existence is the very thing that allows it an uncanny humanity, the very thingness that produces the Thing and thus all of its overcoming of being through the forgetting of time. For the Thing renders itself to us as timeless, we will never get rid of it, and like Poe's famous Raven inside our houses, it's nevermore sounds against the passage of time, and thus ends the passage upon which we have booked our destinies.

Like the sorcerer's apprentice, we are the students of Being. Its power is not yet our own, but through our trial and error we produce the monsters which Goya and others have famously remarked are but the 'dreams the reason': "In fact, *to think of a power means not only to use it, but above all to abuse it.* Were it not for this desire to misuse it, the consciousness of power would not be clearly felt." (Bachelard, op. cit. 78, italics the text's).

The usual moralizing chides us for being 'all too human' in our approach to the infinite, but perhaps this is what is necessary for us as humans, and we can only attain the horizon of Being by suddenly being thrust by our own incautious devices into its arms. Like the realization that we are in love, or even the needful but criminal comprehension that we must 'make love' where it might not actually exist, whether or not the other is willing, this thrusting home of ourselves over the threshold of normative social being both exalts and shames being in the world. The very criminality of unbridled lust helps this process along, though in the moment of its realization we are at pains to understand what it may mean to us later on. Remorse, if it comes at all, is always a reaction: "Anguish arises when the anxious individual is not himself stretched tight by the feeling of superabundance. This is precisely what evinces the isolated, individual character of anguish. There can be anguish only from a personal, *particular* point of view that is radically opposed to the *general*." (Bataille, op. cit. 38-9, italics the text's). If life is inherently overflowing, as Bataille continues, the one who is 'full of it' cannot himself suffer anguish. Thus the exuberance which overflows itself into a conquest of the other is never at risk for an ethical review. It is too full to know itself to still be empty of such things. The absence of reflection within a humanity that partakes of life as such should give us pause, because it is the same feeling of superabundance that allows us the leisurely and unexamined consumption of resources to the 'nth' degree, and thus the ultimate destruction of the world.

There *is* such reflection, but it tends towards a meditation on the *results* of these excesses, which for so long before the advent of modern industrial systems had very little effect on the overall picture. The earth was never in real danger from humanity until quite recently. Such ruminations take the form of warnings more

167

than policy. As with other forms of discourse, it is always easier to mount a criticism than to do something differently, and this itself is also a reflection on the convenience of enjoyment of surplus rather than the sometimes inconvenient storing of surplus for future and needful use. As well, within the caveat discourses of critical modernity, the humanism that is shown there also turns away from itself by relying, sometimes quite heavily, on the previous world-systems of other-worldly soteriology and occluded kerygma: "Strangely, many things reminiscent of the religious tradition emerge in these and other writings, while it is also in some cases clear that they mean to reject religion, at least as it has been understood." (Taylor 2007:321). But such a rejection—e.g. it is the religious construction of the ego in the image of a god that is the true problem of consumption and waste (the world is yours for your uses and the like) as well as the religious notion of the apocalypse that is responsible for our veering towards self-destructive tendencies—is based on the idea that the present can thoroughly extinguish the past, as if the past was no longer a part of itself, like ridding oneself of an ague or complaint that had threatened to become both chronic and thence terminal. It is unlikely that this is the case, first of all, because these agrarian notions are still part of us and will be until the species itself evolves into what could not be called entirely human, and secondly, that for every shady idea that we have inherited from the previous metaphysics there is present too a brighter one that guides our secular salvation. The stewardship of the earth, for instance, or the idea that we are a singular and important part of the cosmos, are such ideas. They too betray the same egotism as the destructive sensibility, and they too will not be overcome —indeed, they are less likely to be so, given their general valuation as goods in themselves—unless and until a new species arises through our co-constructed auto-evolution.

To make the world as it is a meaningful place, the social world is constructed as a symbolic architecture, rich and complex, but with the overarching thematic of attempting to objectivify social relations and personal desires: "Thus the symbol first manifests itself as the killing of the thing, and this death results in the endless perpetuation of the subject's desire." (Lacan 2004:101 [1966]). In terms of cultural evolution, the reconstruction of death in meaningful and symbolic ritual is archaeologically often taken to be the first *symbol* of humanity itself, of our most recent and 'modern' speciation, the doubly wise sub-species of Homo within which we at length have remained. Lacan continues, "The first symbol in which we recognize humanity in its vestiges is the burial, and death as a means can be recognized in every relation in which man is born into the life of his history." (ibid). When we do so, we also over-reach the simple but singular event of death and make it into a symbol of existential freedom. If the funeral is the *first* symbol, it takes the form of symbolization itself. That is, every other act of meaning will have some necessary relation to the new concept of mortality; new because we are unaware ethnographically or archaeologically of another sensibility that we imagine to be more akin to the remaining animal kingdom, where death surely goes unrecognized in the manner in which humanity has attached itself to it: "...the funeral rite presents an act of symbolization par excellence; by means of a forced choice, the subject assumes, repeats his own act, what happened anyway. In the funeral rite, the subject confers the form of a *free* act on an 'irrational' contingent natural process." (Zizek, op. cit. 249). Hence meaningfulness in general will begin to appear to have the power of confronting and combating the lack of sense in the world, or, if the world has its own sensibility, a structure of symbols which is quite apart from human doings, then the world will be considered a creation of another order, in which humans

169

must live, and thus must also make choices rationally to survive within. Whether or not one adheres to creation or evolution as an explanatory schema for the whys and wherefores of human existence, one must come face to face with the character of distanciation inherent in all meaning-making. The desire for death is not to be taken at *face* value. The smugly smirking *rigor mortis* of the moment of death is, on the face of it, a mockery of life, yes, but it is also to be taken as its own warning: Those who only laugh or smile at life whilst alive will suffer the grim fate of not being able to recognize death for what it is. It remains only a symbol and not an authentic terminus. This is so whether or not, once again, one has within one's worldview an afterlife where humanity continues even though consciousness itself is transformed, or where humanity is discontinued by the transformation of matter itself. Rather, we must interpret the desire for death to be in fact a desire for a *meaningful* death, and melancholia or depression rather to the rumination on how, in fact, one can make such a radical event meaningful before it occurs. This is why the melancholic often seems to be rehearsing his own demise, living a living death, as it were. This must be accomplished in advance and cannot be left to those who continue, who succeed our presence in the world. They have their own task—all funerals are for the living—and thus we ourselves take on the task of burying what we are in the meanings of what we had been, our legacies, our 'contributions', our experiences which are uniquely, we imagine, our own. In doing so, we do make a contribution to the general picture of the human condition, to be succeeded and built upon over the passing of generations and to make way for the next question of beings in the world; to get out of the way of the process of Being as the world at large, and to get on with one's own death as a mean to exhort our successors to attend to their own autochthonous business: "The difference for human beings lies in the group character of the selection in question and in their concomitant scope for conscious rational choice of means to advance and secure survival, to reject failures and bequeath knowledge and ideas to their offspring, a faculty characteristic of human evolution." (Blackburn, op. cit. 158). If we are tempted to use our own deaths to utter a final and lasting self-portrait as the grinning ironist, telling the same old joke of the 'lie of life' again and again, we are also just as capable of interpreting and thus exhibiting life in death as a puzzle to be figured out, an aporia to be bridged by the meaningfulness of being able to possess desire at all.

Old World Mind, New World Machine

Yet anyone can follow the path of meditative thinking in his own manner and within his own limits. Why? Because man is a *thinking*, that is, a *meditating* being. Thus meditative thinking need by no means be 'high-flown'. It is enough if we dwell on what lies close and meditate on what is closest; upon that which concerns us, each one of us, here and now; here, on this patch of home ground; now, in the present hour of history. (Heidegger, *Discourse on Thinking*, 1959, page 47).

For many of us, thinking is itself a practical matter. It dwells upon the matters at hand, it lives only for a specific purpose. This because our society provides such ready-mades, the stuff of the collective perception that constitutes a worldview, that in fact we are seldom called upon to think at all. At the same time, perhaps most of us consider thinking to be the province of the scientist or the philosopher alone. For the preeminent thinker of the twentieth century to remind us that this is not at all the case is of great import. It is also quite correct. What the species-essence of humanity is, is thought, made manifest through consciousness. It was once only sentience, billions of years ago, as organic life separated itself from the inorganic fabric of the cosmos. It was once only instinct, when enough complexity accrued through evolutionary organicity to enact the senses protean and proprioceptive. And most recently, it was once only habit; whatever appeared to work was repeated, honed, made second nature.

But in this very process of experiment and experience, thinking presently arose. It was, as it mostly is today, originally geared into the eminent practicality of how to practice a uniquely human life within an anonymous nature. Humans are generalists, we belong to no ecological niche, we adapt to any variable, we shun the specialization of our once closer kindred animals. Even so, thought was itself not yet present. Thinking was a thinking *through*, a thinking *about*, attending to a process or an object problem, and not a thinking-in-itself, thought for the sake of thought alone. This final aspect of consciousness as we know it is what can be called 'meditative' thinking. It differs from Eastern forms of meditation, wherein thinking in the Western sense is to be temporarily expunged. This more well-known definition of meditation remains a healthy exercise for the mind and body alike, but it serves the futurity of our species-being only insofar as it sets up a contrast between what consciousness is when it becomes less active; outwardly more like a lower form of life – a sensory apparatus that only reacts – and inwardly perhaps more like one higher – the Gods have no need of thought as all is already known to them.

But meditating upon an abstract problem, including the perennial 'problem of consciousness', an ontological puzzle, or even the 'problem of knowledge', an epistemological issue, is quite different than 'meditation' in the spiritual sense, transcendental or otherwise. It is the idea that one can *have* an idea that prompts the sense that I as a human being am capable of thought. Not that 'my idea' is prone to any singular possession. Anything we do is automatically the proof property of the species at large. Even if we tell no one, it influences our acts, our further thoughts. In a word, I am altered in my very being by having *this* thought, as I am created as a thrown project by having thought itself.

Yet if thinking is not the province of the philosopher alone, why then do we have so many occasions to note its relative absence in the world? If anyone can participate, why then do we not see more interest in this regard? The most authentic challenge to thinking comes from our need to think *about* the world. We imagine that our 'patch of home ground' is indeed what is 'closest to us'. The exhortation to 'act locally but think globally' is a noble one, nonetheless, it simply substitutes a smaller concern *in* the world for the world *as* a concern. Both are objects in this sense, and thus even if their scale differs, they remain quantities, *things*, about which we attempt to negotiate or 'figure out'. The sense that something either works or it does not promotes a thinking that is sustainable only within the context of work, and increasingly, simple labor. Let me use the obvious contraption 'thing-king' to designate this kind of thought process. In thing-king, there is a beginning and an end, and both are precise enough to ingratiate a practice that may, over time, become a personal habit or yet a cultural habitus. We notice a problem, issue, challenge, or mistake. This is the start of practical thought, thinking about a thing. 'Fixing' the issue is the only goal. Many means may be necessary, certainly, but the end is defined at the beginning and as Heidegger's student Arendt has cautioned, we cannot 'justify' separating ends and means in the trite manner of the moral chestnut simply because the ends have *already* delineated the means and therefore have by definition 'justified' them ahead of time.

Not that this is necessarily an ethical problem pending the ends. By far most everyday challenges require no revolutionary means to achieve a desired outcome. They neither demand the radical nor the novel. They are simply part and parcel of ordinary existence and remain within a logistics of worldliness. It is in this way, even though they are deemed to be necessities of human life, that such practicalities prevent thinking from arising. That this is an authentic bracketing of thought is evidenced by the lifeworld's insistence upon its own reproduction. We cannot think in a void. But practice – the fixing of logistical issues, the enactment of means tending toward finite goals which can be known or at least observed from a short distance – and even praxis – the sense that practical theory is itself a means to world-historical action – do not suffice, and can never suffice, for thought itself. For thinking, as opposed to thing-king, is encountered, not enacted. Its goals are undefined ahead of time, its means are diffuse and seemingly have a life of their own. Thinking is, in a word, *about* nothing other than thoughts and thus takes place only within the history of consciousness.

So while it is reasonable to exclaim at this juncture that, 'I have no time to meditate on abstractions, things that aren't really things at all. I have to get on with it', we must ask the question, 'what, exactly, does getting on with things mean, suggest, imply?' At once we have our genuine response: human life is composed chiefly of activities that from time to time need to be adjusted to practical purpose and to finite ends. Even so, the truth of this statement is only the case within a wider understanding of existence, one that includes, and indeed is originated by, our species-essential ability to think at all. Practice and praxis alike represent means only, and whatever 'ends' that are contained within this or that process of such thing-king are themselves but further means.

But means to what? Meditative or contemplative *thinking is its own end insofar as it is a means to itself.* This may sound circular as well as pompous, but consider thinking with the understanding that thought is neither a subject alone – our thoughts are historical, factual, mythical, as well as being biographical; but then again, what is so much of our biography if not habitus made *into* habit? – nor is it an object – thinking is very much *not* a thing in the physical sense, and attempts to reduce thought to neurochemical combinations and synaptic structures only serve to place the process by which thought arises into some more precise locales. Given our human success is due to our ability to 'think things through', the sense that we should try to locate thought as if it were *itself* a thing seems counterintuitive, for our thinking mimics our wider heritage as evolutionary generalists. We are potentially unlimited as a species, even if I as an individual must meditate 'within my limits'. This is the more profound meaning of the near and the far to be found in sudden declamations to 'think globally, act locally' and so on. I act and think within certain limits, many of them not my own in any individuated sense, yet I can also at least imagine thinking, if not truly acting, in a much wider way. It is that single act of imagination which allows us to encounter the essence of thinking-as-it-is.

Yet if there is an uneasy, even somewhat suspicious relationship between practice and thought, the one still admits to the other that its practices originate in contemplative thinking. It is otherwise with the inauthentic barriers to meditative thought that our everyday world has constructed. These include the distractions of the newer lifeworld of the idolatrous thing, the fetishized commodity, but as well, the delusions of the older lifeworld's customs and rituals, what is defined as habitus and heresy alike. Between the machine of the new and the mind of the old, human thinking is confined to a space stenochoric to the future and at once reduced to peering at a thin slice of the past. Custom represents only the most common elements of culture, no matter if this or that ritual comes once in an individual lifetime. And the technology of a culture in turn represents what is most commonly practiced by those same individuals. Both rely upon repetition, and only challenge us when the outcomes expected from them do not automatically materialize.

Even when this is the case, 'fixing it' immediately becomes the end to which the means at hand are harnessed. There can be no thought outside of these circles, whether sacred or secular, whether customary or technological. But meditative thinking is neither sacred nor secular, it engages no loyalty to religion revealed or 'civil', and in this lies the key to our encounter with it: *thinking is itself revolutionary*. By this I mean that in order to engage in thinking as a species-essential gift and task, one must needs shed *all* loyalties to both custom and craft. One must begin to understand means and ends as artificial boundaries that impede the act of thought by reducing it to a specific point-to-point process. There is no 'there' to thinking, as Heidegger has implied. It is a here and now encounter with the new and with my ownmost being which is ever new. *This* is what is closest to us; our own being in the world as I breathe and as I am. Yes, this existence precedes an understanding of essence but it does not negate it, in the same manner as though we have historically given ourselves credit for the death of the Gods and the shattering of the illusory otherworld, does not then mean that otherness no longer exists.

For thinking is itself *other*. It is other to life as we have known it, to history as it has been, to myself as I know myself and what I expect from myself. It is other to what is customary, but also to what is technical and of technique alone. It is other to the generalized otherness of the social fabric and it thus gifts us with the ongoing task of being more than we have taken ourselves to be and to once have been. The old world mind is an *unthought vice* of tradition alone, unchallenged and too well known to aid the human future, while the new world machine is an *unthinking device* which cannot know itself and thus has no future. Only human thought, meditative and contemplative, abruptly present and yet in the ever-closing presence of the future, opening us to the possibilities of consciousness in its relationship with the cosmos from which it has perhaps unexpectedly sprung, marks us as worthy of a continued existence.

The State of the Division Address

I speak to you today from an unknown location. This place which has no name, and which can only be called therefore a space, is nothing less than the Now. It is immanent; it is fullest presence. It calls to the conscience and yet must defer its response to the future. This future does not yet exist and yet it in turn is imminent, almost upon us. It is simply what is next, and because we cannot entirely know the next thing, event, time or place, its import escapes us. Living as humans within the ambit of mortal consciousness, knowing the past exists as memory, trace, artifact and history; knowing the present is too fleeting to dwell within; and knowing that the future is itself unknowing of its own presence, it is perhaps inevitable that we turn elsewhere to understand the meaning of our condition, odd and fragile.

Even though each one of us exists simultaneously in all three guises of abstract time – we have memories and we live in cultures which have histories; we are 'in' the moment without being inside of it as if we were halted and time had stopped; and we design our lives so that a future of some kind is expected if not entirely taken for granted – and thus each of us understands, however incompletely, the indwelling of our beings in that unknown location which nevertheless speaks to us of existence *itself*, it has become clear that we as a mass culture have limned ourselves into an unenviable position regarding the definition of this 'elsewhere' to which we direct all of our collective energies.

The choice laid before us is one between two further abstractions, freedom and salvation. They are opposites, even antagonists, and their hold upon our imagination is such that if we do decide for one or the other, the one left to the side is immediately scrabbled up as if it too were part of the singular decision; being saved first is also being free, being free first is thence being saved. Because these two conceptions refer to states of being and their relationship to Being, whatever the definition of this may be – it matters only for the ethnographer to delineate the contents of belief; here it is a question of contrasting absolute values of faith – it is always possible to add to one's choice an indefinite list of other traits which are claimed to accrue to the original state. One thus finds ultimate freedom in an intimacy with a Being and a history which offers salvation of beings, or one finds that one has saved oneself, not only from the History of Being as an alternative and oft-seen superior ontology, but also from the very much human history that is just as often understood to have been a conflict sourced in beliefs *about* Being. So, on the one side, salvation offers an exeunt from our mortality; it is the finitude which hallmarks historical consciousness uplifted into the infinitude which expresses the continuity between Man and God. The cosmos presents to us no longer a finite experience, but one more in line with its own cycle of infinity. On the other side, finitude is accepted as a celebration of the open future in which anything may occur and through which I may become anything I desire, thereby placing me within the infinitude of cosmic evolution. My finite existence has become infinite through my participation in that ongoingness which in its totality must escape my partial imagination. In this very incompleteness do I find my ultimate freedom, since I have no reason nor ability to know the whole.

Both of these absolute values are powerful expressions of the will to life. Salvation seeks life eternal and thus the overcoming of both will and history. Freedom desires a will that is itself endless, hooked into both human history and that cosmic. I marvel at both senses of *how* we are *what* we are; a consciousness made up of an ethical conscience, a reasoning wide-awake thinking, and an uncannily clever unconscious which, contrary to some popular psychological accounts as well as old-world demonologies, tirelessly works wholly in the service *of* that very reason. Once again, while salvation seemingly offers sanctity to being, freedom appears to offer it sanity. The difference lies in one's willingness to frame will and faith either together as sibling allies, or as contiguous but contrasting interests and drives. Salvation unites will and faith by subsuming will as the worldly manifestation and agent of faith. Freedom unites both by defining them as almost the same thing; one must have faith *in* one's will, for instance, and one must will oneself to *have* faith in the face of both an impersonal though intimate history, and a cosmos both anonymous and aloof. Salvation tells us that we are not alone in our quest for the wisdom, not of the 'how', but of the *why*, while freedom declares that our solitude is at the very heart of authentic choice and the being-able of living as a reasoning being. It takes the presence of human reason to be evidence of our evolutionary ability to free ourselves *from* that very evolution. Salvation seeks to convince us that this ability is the kerygmatic gift of a God; bestowed upon us so that we can know of God's will and perhaps even of God's mind. Freedom assures us that the Gestalt of the entire history and pre-history of our species is contained within that same kernel; our ability to think things through with no end is thus just as infinite as is the mind of any divinity.

So is it an effort merely of perspective to offer ourselves these two ultimate sensibilities? Are we describing to ourselves the converse side of the same shining object, the brilliance emanating therefrom blinding us to the reality that it is the *same* thing of which we are speaking? If this is indeed the case, then we have defined both salvation and freedom only incompletely, using the other as a foil and as counterpoint, when in fact they are two names for the same basic will to live and live on. At present, from our unknown mortal space, we can only suggest that this may be the most reasonable manner to think about them. In doing so, we avoid placing them in competition with one another and we may even be able to use each one as a way of understanding the manifold of the other. This is not a purely historical exercise, in that we are not solely interested in questions such as 'how did the concept of freedom change or limit that of salvation?' or 'how does the lingering belief in salvation impact or impinge upon our conception of freedom?' and the like. No, such a question that brings together salvation and freedom in a tandem query about the *meaning* of being-present, currently unknown, states at once the division in our contemporary culture and a manner through which it can be partially overcome. It tells us why we *are so* divided, which in itself is a kind of Godsend, as well as expressing a doubly powerful means by which we can understand one another with a great deal more authenticity and intimacy than we currently do.

For right now, the extended presence of the Now in both directions, as it were, we are nothing *but* division, and the boundary drawn up in the sand beneath and between us is inscribed by the hand of a being who has taken on for itself either the divine or the cosmic. In both we are utterly mistaken about our condition. In reality, we are neither the authors of salvation nor of freedom, for we are but expressions, in both narratives, of either a superior being which is Being 'itself', or another order of being which encompasses all beings. To pretend to either is to at best avoid our status as the 'one who can think but not know', the 'one who can reason through unreason' - referring to the interface between the conscious mind and that unconscious – and the 'one which lives on in spite of death'. Neither the divine nor the cosmic has any use for such devices as we have conjured for ourselves, so in dividing I and thou, I am not only doing a disservice to that mortal genius I am also dragging the infinite down to my small level. Only in my narrow imagination does it concede and consent.

Instead, this state of the current division in our global society should inform us that we are dangerously near the precipice which heralds the loss of *all* meaning. In placing overmuch the value of absolution into absolute terms, both the purveyor of salvation and that of freedom have excerpted themselves from their own shared humanity. In spite of the historical argument that salvation speaks to us of something that has always been and is itself timeless, whereas freedom recognizes that the essence of time is tempered only through temporality and thus cannot be overtaken by Being, it is more truly a question of whether or not there is to *be* a human future. In this, salvation steps aside from the ongoingness of the imminent future, and freedom seeks to influence, even control, its oncoming mass. Salvation pulls me out of its way, freedom allows me to step bodily into it. More truly then, the apparent choice to be made between the two absolute values is one of ethics. Do I take myself out of history entirely, that passed and that yet to be made, or do I throw myself once more into the flux through which I have also lived? Is this a choice for the moment, or is it rather that we are staring in the face of the very passage to Being? In a word, that we must choose freedom first and let salvation happen in due course, that freedom is in fact a choice and salvation is simply an outcome? It is too trite to simply tell ourselves that 'heaven can wait', for in imagining that something *other* is indeed awaiting us takes the edge away from living being; that double-sided edge, one of which we own as a visionary sword and the other of which threatens us at every mortal turn. No, just here we must step back and honestly answer to our ownmost condition: I *cannot* know of my own salvation; I *cannot* avoid my own freedom. So the very choice between absolute values is itself a false one. Spurious and specious, both salvation and freedom, one the unknowing fraud of premodernity and the other the overwrought charade of our own time, have combined to render human existence too partial to its own projections. The time has come to place both to the side and step away from the disunity they have sowed amongst our shared humanity. Only by doing so will we have an opportunity to discover that if and in the first place, *either* of them were ever real.

Modernity's Fragile Selfhood

Here there speaks no fanatic, here there is no 'preaching', here *faith* is not demanded; out of an infinite abundance of light and depth of happiness there falls drop after drop, word after word – a tender slowness of pace is the tempo of these discourses. Such things as this reach only the most select... (Nietzsche, 1888).

In his foreword to his final work, completed mere weeks before his genetic neurological condition overtook him, Nietzsche's absolute affirmation of personal character in the face of the fate modernity had proclaimed upon itself is yet mitigated by its reliance, albeit indirect, upon the very antithesis to his own philosophy, that of the 'tragic recurrence'. This is so because to affirm the self as 'what one must become and what one is' is to take seriously the ancient notion of the intrinsic value of the self and of each person's selfhood. Nietzsche's anti-Christian and anti-Buddhist sentiments are not sabotaged by this ethical kinship, but rather made into obverses thereof, for the Nietzschean self hypostasizes the selfhood first introduced in the East and then the West by these then novel world-systems. But we must ask first, what *is* this radical affirmation of being-oneself working against, given that by the time of the *fin de siècle* no antique religion could have had such suasion to prompt the much touted 'reevaluation of all values'.

Let us then suggest that Nietzsche's target is not religion at all, but rather everything that at first denied and then overcame the religious sense of both selfhood and fate alike. It is well known that Nietzsche, though he accepted Darwin's understanding of the origins of life as a fact, was most dismayed by its discovery. That evolution during the nineteenth century was seen as a radical denial of creation – today, we realize that cosmic evolution must understand itself, with a certain irony to be sure, very much in the cast of the old metaphysics; infinite in terms of the cyclical universe or yet the multiverse: there is no 'starting point'; both of these are ancient ideas that pre-date by far the religions of intrinsically valuable selfhood – suggested to Nietzsche the idea that God was now 'dead'. Discursively, such an 'event' must be back-dated at least to Hume and Vico, who between them relativized the conception of both culture and history and hence as well all contents as might be found within these. However unwitting this murder may have been in the 1730s, by the 1880s the divine corpse had been retrieved and the mourning begun.

But Nietzsche asks, what is, *who* is Man without God? 'Man' too, now lives on borrowed time and indeed, 1914 put an end to the culture which exonerated mankind from its undue and vain fixation upon the sense that progress and evolution not only went hand in hand but were more or less the *same* thing. In our own time, beginning in the 1920s, the personalization of religion was undertaken in earnest. Today, the conception of God is as is the conception of Man; for Western believers, God is one's *own* God, and each of us is said to have a 'personal' connection to such a divinity that was utterly unknown historically. Conversely, 'Man' has become 'men', or, more politic, 'humanity'. Because of its indubitable link with organismic evolution, the term humanity has within it an undeniable species reference and thus is difficult for many people to identify with. It seems to denote our *animal* form, though at a distance from nature, rather than connote the spirit which was understood as *animating* that form. As such, our contemporary conception of ourselves does not make up for the loss of the divine definition of the locus of our being.

And this is, in essence, the entire issue within the ineptly named 'culture wars'. There is nothing within modernity that can equal, let alone better, the ancient understanding of humanity as divinely endowed, not just with grace, but also with reason. And Nietzsche was the first thinker to realize this. In the face of this insoluble problem which he also understood as inevitable, he offered instead the absolute affirmation of the self-as-it-is: Godless, finite, but subject to the eternal recurrence of the same and constantly willing itself into being through 'the will to power and nothing besides', as he famously intones. It is a bold, courageous and altogether necessary maneuver, but can it ever be more than a 'quick fix'? Nietzsche's 'Dionysian' tone, especially vivid in his final works, implies that it cannot in fact be anything more. What was 'more' was lost forever when humanity decided to make decisions for itself, by itself. This condition was foreshadowed in the Hebrew account of the expulsion. To speak somewhat metaphorically, what the serpent didn't count on was being ejected along *with* the unhappy couple and thence was also left to fend for itself. Evil, in a word, had thus also been personalized.

With the individuation of both good and evil it could only be a matter of time before the entire system that was constructed by the moral apparatus of a great chain of being broke apart. It was given impetus, certainly, by the 'discovery' of global cultures of which no canonical narrative could take account. The 'lost tribe' sensibility carried one only so far. *How* many lost tribes, again? Beyond this, the perduring resistance to any specific world-system by its competitors – today, the half billion plus Buddhists number the very smallest of the four major religious oriented architectures, for instance – frustrated any attempt to argue that one specific faith had actually latched on, even by happenstance, to the truth of things. And beyond this, the rise of scientific method and result, conquering the vast majority of explanatory territory that used to be the sole preserve of religious explication, ultimately felled the now hollow idols that Nietzsche, in an almost reminiscent manner, discusses in *Götzendammerung* (also written in 1888). All of these world historical factors occurred, however, long before Nietzsche was writing anything at all, and it is a simple error of displacement to associate his work with the reality of our mutable, if loosely shared, condition, either at present or centuries ago.

Instead, Nietzsche today looks more like an ally for a kind of morality than anything else. The ethics of the 'Overman' are their own super-morality, one to which the finite and discontinuous beings of a humanity made base by evolution might aspire. But we cannot be naïve on such a profound score; the path before us is not one of a humanity evolving into something which is 'beyond' itself. This sensibility echoes the tradition, wherein transfiguration was an active mechanic. Today, the desperate rush to invent an 'indefinite human', a cyber-organic-stem-celled-artificially-intelligent 'thing', is a symptom not of aspiration at all, but rather of anxiety. And it is not death *per se* that animates this inauthentic anxiety, but rather, and once again, vanity. It is almost as if the brash among us say to themselves, "If God has been dead, perhaps even since the incarnation – this is why the Father left the Son 'hanging', so to speak; the former was already dead – and now Man as well has passed, then those remaining are destined to become the *new* divinities"; 'Men as Gods', to borrow Wells' title. Vanity, yes, but also a kind of neurotic compulsion to mechanically metastasize mortal desire unto infinity.

Nothing against the passions, we must note. They have their place, especially for youth, as part of a phase of ever-changing human existence, even within the singular life. But obsession denies that life, just as delusion obfuscates the life of the species-essence more generally. For a mature being, the very definition of growth is to place each phase's form of being within its own existential envelope, and desire, anxiousness, even recklessness, all 'the passions unabated', as Goethe has it, belong with youth and to youth alone they must adhere. A great scandal of modernity is, to my mind, how we have extended youth indefinitely – it is surely our own 'adult' fetishization of youth, something we ourselves have lost, that motivates us not only to keep youth young for overlong as well as imagine being ourselves eternally young as a consciousness housed in a future machine – at the cost of other phases of the human experience. We hear of evangelicals coercing young adults as if they were still small children, including physically coercing them in certain sects. And though this is deplorable, to focus our critique upon it alone is a mere decoy and projection, exuding from us, and as such constitutes a denial of how the larger society seeks to keep *all* persons childish, ideally for the entire life-course, simply because we are more easily manipulatable in that form. We can thus be sold almost anything, from irrelevant toys to equally irrelevant, but all the more dangerous, politicians.

So Nietzsche's exhortation must also be seen as an argument against *any* sense of 'beyond' at all, whether one traditional or one hypermodern. The Overman is manifestly *not* a superior being in terms of mechanism or dispassion. Rather it is the maturity of being that recognizes that existential change over the life course is our way of 'dying many times to become immortal'. No zealot, no 'fanatic', speaks of or to this kind of being. Within its changing course, we are as is the neighbor figure; spontaneous, shunning the status and esteem of social role, reaching out to others in distress as by self-definition and as a creative ethics. Hence there is also no sermon, no 'preaching', of such a spontaneity. It is as we are, thrown into the world very much *against* our individual will. Indeed, one could still argue with some merit that this existential thrownness – none of us asks to be born and this is as well why no 'faith' as such is required, at least at first – bears the imprint of the afterlife of all Godhead, or perhaps it could be experienced as a kind of 'afterglow'; life as the outcome of what remains an astonishing miracle of birth. And we are, sectarian or no, *all* of us born again and again over the life course, if we allow ourselves to be so. Those who are lucky enough to grow old accomplish this marvelous feat, with more or less elegance and aplomb, and with it begin to know the truer grace of Being as self-created in the face of the void.

Notes

i   The individual plays a strong and semi-voluntaristic role in the apparent omnipotence and omniscience of governmental authority, certainly when the regime is transparently authoritarian, but no doubt all the more so when it is not, given that no ruling body can be all places at all times. Gadamer speaks of this during the Nazi period: "What a tragedy it is that we have these demagogues and their unscrupulous band of followers governing us! And there was the Gestapo, whose omniscience we probably overestimated. That I admit. We all had a part in spreading the terror by overestimating the knowledge the Gestapo had. We believed they knew everything." (2001:126).

ii   Speaking of a number of conservative historians in the former West Germany, Bosworth relates how the claims of Habermas against this group publicized the problem of 'relative revisionism' of the recent past: "The purpose of their pact was exhibited both in new museums of Bonn and West Berlin and in a number of recent books and articles. What was planned was a re-minted German nationalism, which would explain Nazism away and re-connect present-day Germany with a glorious past. As part of that process, both Nazism and the Holocaust were to be relativised." (1997:82). Hitler's ultimately reckless military adventures against the East were to be seen as justified given Stalin's more 'original' purges and atrocities and the danger of a rampant and suffocating Stalinism in Europe.

iii   These more recent and completely political fetishes of course come in many forms, some which Spencer and others would not necessarily have foreseen, just as Marx may have not had in mind the advent of modern advertising in the mid-1920s at the precise moment that over-production was attained. The ideal realm too has its over-productions, wherein real drama is turned to unreal or surreal melodrama. Cole reminds us that the theologian Neusner suggested that the Holocaust became mythic somewhere around the 1967 war and it was in the USA where this first occurred: "His argument is that in 1967 American Jews took hold of the Holocaust in direct response to the geo-political situation in Israel, and created 'the American Judaism of Holocaust and Redemption. This - Neusner suggests - involved 'the transformation of the mass murder of European Jews into an event of mythic and world destroying proportions'." (1999:9).

iv The individual is subsumed in both forms. In the first, as a real likeness of his actual neighbor, as one who is very much what the other is, as members of the same clan or totem, for instance, or kinship group or village. In the second, unlike persons must conform to the laws of citizenship and can only derive an identity within the framework of the state: "This way of thinking is not opposed to Marxism; it is different, however, in that it gives the state the preponderant and definite place that Hegel gave it. Man as defined by the Hegelian idea is not an individual, but the state. The individual has died in it, has been absorbed into the higher reality and into the service of the state; in a wider sense, the 'statesman' is the sea into which flows the rivers of history. Insofar as he participates in the state, man leaves both animality and individuality behind him: He is no longer separate from universal reality." (Bataille, 1988:151-2 [1967]). It is this cosmic ordering of human relations which is the ultimate symbol of unity, and the ultimate value, good or evil, to which humanity either aspires of desires to avoid.

v Even in our most primordial imaginations, otherness was something to be extinguished and avoided: "Archaic societies, societies of the mark, are societies without a State, *societies against the State*. The mark on the body, on all bodies alike, declares: *You will not have the desire for power; you will not have the desire for submission*. And that non-separate law can only have for its inscription a space that is not separate: that space is the body itself." (Clastres, op. cit. 188, italics the text's).

References

Adorno, Theodor
> 1998 *Critical Models - interventions and catchwords.* Columbia, New York. [1969].

Bataille, Georges
> 1991 *The Accursed Share, volumes two and three.* Zone Books. New York. [1976].
> 1988 *The Accursed Share, volume one.* Zone Books, New York. [1967].

Acton-Dahlberg, Lord
> 1906 *Lectures on Modern History.* Macmillan and Co, London. (1960)

Bachelard, Gaston
> 1964 *The Psychoanalysis of Fire.* Beacon Press, Boston. [1938].

Blackburn, Richard James
> 1990 *The Vampire of Reason: an essay in the philosophy of history.* Verso, New York.

Bosworth, R.J.B.
> 1993 *Explaining Auschwitz and Hiroshima: history writing and the second world war 1945-1990.* Routledge, London.

Brierley, Marjorie
> 1951 *Trends in Psychoanalysis.* The Hogarth Press and the Institute of Psychoanalysis. London.

Burton, Robert

1938 *The Anatomy of Melancholy*. Tudor Publishing Company, New York. [1651].

Cassirer, Ernst

1946 *The Myth of the State*. Yale. New Haven.

Clastres, Pierre

1987 *Society Against the State*. Zone Books, New York. [1974].

Cole, Tim

1999 *Selling the Holocaust: from Auschwitz to Schindler – how history is bought, packaged, and sold*. Routledge, London.

De Sade, Marquis

1966 *The 120 Days of Sodom and other writings*. Grove, New York. [1785].

Derrida, Jacques

2001 *The Work of Mourning*. The University of Chicago Press, Chicago.

Feyerabend, Paul K.

1987 *Against Method*. Verso, New York.

Freud, Sigmund

1957 *Collected Papers Volume 3*.

Gadamer, Hans-Georg

2001 *Gadamer in Conversation - reflections and commentary*. Yale, New Haven.

1998 *Praise of Theory - speeches and essays*. Yale, New Haven. [1983].

Gellner, Ernest

1985 *Relativism and the Social Sciences*. Cambridge University Press, Cambridge

Glass, James
1997   *"Life Unworthy of Life"* - *racial phobia and mass murder in Hitler's Germany.* Basic Books, New York

Heidegger, Martin
1959   *Discourse on Thinking.* Harper and Row, New York (1966).

Horowitz, Gregg M.
2001   *Sustaining Loss: art and mournful life.* Stanford University Press, Stanford.

James, William
1902   *The Variety of Religious Experience: a study in human nature.* Longmans, London.

Lacan, Jacques
2004   *Ecrits: a selection.* Norton, New York. [1966].

Mendel, Sydney
1974   *Roads to Consciousness.* George Allen and Unwin, London.

Merleau-Ponty, Maurice
1955   *Adventures in the Dialectic.* Northwestern University Press, Evanston. (1973).

Nietzsche, Friedrich
1969   *Ecce Homo.* Penguin, London. (1888 [1908]).
1974   *The Will to Power.* Vintage, New York. (1880s-[1900]).

Pike, Kenneth L.
1957   *Language in Relation to a Unified Theory of the Structure of Human Behavior.* Mouton, The Hague.

Ricoeur, Paul
1955   *History and Truth.* Northwestern University Press, Evanston. (1973).

Scheler, Max

    1912-3 *Ressentiment.* Marquette University Press, Milwaukee (2003).

Sontag, Susan

    1978 *Illness as Metaphor.* Vintage Books, New York. Spencer, Herbert

    1940 *The Man Versus the State.* Caxton Printers, Caldwell, Idaho. [1892].

Taylor, Charles

    2007 *A Secular Age.* Harvard University Press, Cambridge, MA.

Zizek, Slavoj

    1990 *The Sublime Object of Ideology.* Verso, New York. [1989].

Review Requested:

We'd like to know if you enjoyed the book.
Please consider leaving a review on the platform
from which you purchased the book.

CPSIA information can be obtained
at www.ICGtesting.com
Printed in the USA
LVHW111203271022
731696LV00001B/129